Everlasting Grace

Shirley,

May God's Everlasting Grace
fill your heart with His
Love Always

Everlasting Grace

MIRACULOUS ENCOUNTERS WITH GOD

SALLY ANN QUINONES

For copies: www.SallyAnnQuinones.com

Publishing consulting and production:
Aimazing Publishing & Marcom, Phoenix, AZ
www.aimazingpmc.com

Art Credits:
Holy Sacraments: Illustrated by Pat Wilke Tadena
Starburst/rays image, used in cover, by Flávio Takemoto

ISBN 978-0-615-41408-9

❧

Dedication

I dedicate this book to my mother and father,
who both have gone to heaven to be with the Lord.
They taught us as family, "We are our brother's keeper."

To my children Cynthia, Esther, Jeana,
Shelby, and Rudy Jr.
You have supported me throughout my journey of faith.
You have laughed with me and cried with me
throughout my walk with the Lord.

To my twenty grandchildren and two
great-granddaughters, all of whom I am so proud.
You have brought so much love and joy to my life.

To my sisters Francis, Louise, and Mary,
and my brother Louis Jr.
Thank you for all your support throughout my life.
I was able to share my visions with you, and you believed.

And to my sister Carmen who is a devout Jehovah's Witness.
We might not share the same faith, but we all came
from the same family.
"We are the six-million dollar clan."

To all my friends whom the Lord has brought into my life
here in Arizona, in Florida, and California.
You all are treasures to me.

❧

Acknowledgments

I wish to express my gratitude to Scandia Hefta, a young woman whom I met at Arizona Home Care. The first time I spoke to her, she was at the printer. I asked her how she was, and she replied, "Tired." She went on to say that she worked two jobs. I asked what she did at her other job, and she said, "data entry," and mentioned that she typed one hundred twenty words a minute. I immediately asked, "How would you like a third job? I have been journaling and hand writing many stories throughout the years, and now I feel it is time to write a book about my experiences, but I need a fast typist to transfer them into my computer." Scandia agreed to come on Saturdays and, in just six weeks, had everything entered. I can still hear her typing away. She was extremely fast and committed. I don't know anyone else who could have done this for me in such a short time. Thank you, Scandia.

Then there is Julie Artesi who came from Stockton, California, and stayed with me for a week to help me put the first chapter together. She continued to help me by editing my stories through e-mail. Julie is the one who kept encouraging me to continue to put the chapters together. She would always tell me, "This is going to be a good book. It will glorify the Lord." Julie has been my friend for many years and has been a great motivator. She always told me, "You can do anything you put your mind to do, Sally."

I can't forget to thank Erin O'Brien, a woman I met through the Monday night prayer meetings at Queen of Peace Parish in Mesa, AZ. After sharing one of my stories with the group, I mentioned that I was putting a book together but it still needed a lot of work. Erin approached me and said, "I have a master's degree in English; could I be of any help to you?" What a blessing! Erin came to my house on Saturdays and she, too, edited many of the stories.

My deep appreciation goes to Vince and Mary Aflague for funding my book. This is how God's everlasting grace flowed through them to make it possible for this book to be published. On Sunday, April 11, 2010, at five o'clock in the morning, I was at the St. Peregrine Shrine, which is on the campus of my parish, Christ the King in Mesa, Arizona. Each week I spend an hour in adoration before the Blessed Sacrament and pray for my family and friends and those who have asked for my prayers. That morning, after praying for everyone, I said, "Now it is my turn to ask for your help, Lord. My prayer to you is this: If you want this book to be published, you must help me get it funded. I'm going to put it in your hands." I also said, "Blessed Mother, let Jesus know that I need the money to come from Him."

Later that morning, as I left my house to attend eleven o'clock Mass, I realized I had forgotten my glasses. When I came back inside the house, the phone was ringing. My friend Mary Aflague was calling to invite me to lunch and to request a registration form for our parish's upcoming Christ Renews His Parish weekend retreat. After lunch, Mary filled out the form, and then her husband, Vince, asked me about my book and how it was coming along. I told him it was finally finished except for the funds. He said, "Sally, Mary and I want to fund your book." He asked what it would cost, asked Mary for the checkbook, and wrote a check to cover the cost. I was truly at a loss for words and thought, *I just asked the Lord for the money this morning and already I have it!* After giving these dear friends my heartfelt thanks, I drove right back to the shrine to thank God for His everlasting grace. Vince and Mary, I pray that God will continue to bless you both and answer all your prayers.

I have my friend Mary Riley to thank for making it possible to meet with Bonnie Crutcher, Aimazing Publishing & Marcom, at a restaurant in Scottsdale, AZ. It was there I handed Bonnie the rough draft of my manuscript. I felt that her knowledge and experience would change that rough draft into a beautiful book. Thank you, Bonnie, for pulling it all together and making the necessary changes while always thinking of my voice as the writer. Thanks to you, my stories will be better understood by the reader. I give thanks to God for the time you devoted to make this dream come true. My family and I will always remember you, and we will pray that God will shower his grace upon you and your family always.

Contents

❦

Foreword 1

When Sally Ann asked me if I would write a brief foreword for this wonderful book you are holding in your hands, I smiled and readily accepted with great honor, faith, and obedience. Honor, because once you finish reading these amazing stories, you will understand what great honor comes from just knowing Sally. Faith, because Sally, like many devoted Christians who have ever lived or are alive today, did not listen to the secular voices of adversity, claiming, "It's not possible...." On the contrary, Sally believes that all things are possible with God and so precedes with a gentle boldness and a childlike confidence, which most of us have lost long ago. Most important, I was happy to respond out of obedience, because our Lord has bestowed Sally with a great gift of revelation. How could I refuse His messenger? I smile as I type these words, realizing that, well, brief and foreword should not be used in the same sentence when discussing any spiritual matter involving or describing Sally, because with Sally, the matter is always spiritual.

I met Sally in 1985, at a clinical laboratory in Stockton, California. I was her supervisor, and she was my most peculiar employee. I clearly recall when she first turned to look at me through long dark lashes, her big brown eyes filled with joy, how she embraced my forearm as if I were a long lost friend. Her exuberance, her unwavering joy, her perpetual and most enigmatic smile made me wonder if something was wrong with her. I'm sad to say I even found her excessive kindness and glorious reverential singing, "How great thou art—how great thou art—hum, hum—how great thou art...." most annoying. She did not know all the words and could not carry a tune— but NO—that did not stop Sally from singing praises while cramped in her cubicle. I used to think *okay, okay, enough with the singing and get to work,* but I just could not bring myself to silence her praises. In fact, I recall many moments cringing, wide-eyed, with furrowed brow, and biting the corner of my lower lip to refrain from sighing, bemoaning, exhaling—ugh. To make matters worse, Sally constantly shuffled her rosary beads over her work surface, which interrupted my concentration on tasks at hand.

At this point, you may wonder why Sally would ask ME to write her foreword. The answer is very clear and simple. I am no longer a stoic, lost little lamb, and I do not know anyone who has spent time with Sally who has not been affected, rather converted, by her humble nature and her amazing gift of grace.

During the brief time Sally and I worked together, she constantly said, "I'm just not smart. Oh, I can't do that...," shaking her head, "...but I'm not a fast learner, I'm sorry...." I confidently responded, "Oh, you can do anything; you're much smarter than you think!" and handed her a large batch of Medicare claims. A look of concern crossed her face, and she appeared to mumble a prayer.

I walked away knowing that somehow Sally would become one of my most ardent employees. My peripheral vision caught a glow around her. *Was this a figment of my imagination?* I disregarded the event. Sally not only succeeded in manually billing the entire batch of claims but also continued to outperform in all assigned tasks.

As I reflect on those early years, I now realize that because Sally responds in great faith to God's call, He duly rewards her. Sally is an example of seeking first the Kingdom of God and believing all things will be given unto you. She never asks, "How can this be?" She asks, "What Lord? Your servant is listening."

Now, finally, the time has come for the unveiling of her life's testimony, so you too will know that His Grace is sufficient. The following stories compiled in this book unveil extraordinary experiences that may prompt you to recall those infamous words, "For those who believe, no explanation is necessary. For those who do not believe, no explanation is possible."

As you read the following pages, you will hear Sally's voice vary as that of the erudite "dumb ox"[1], with an occasional kick from an affable donkey,[2] and every now and then you will hear the whisper of a little flower[3]. Oh, and there is a hint of that stern, yet humble friar[4] who keeps a stronghold in the periphery—guarding, guiding, giving.

One must read Sally's words with great faith for that is the only way one can sing praises to our Father who has, "…hidden these things from the wise and the prudent, and hast revealed them to little ones."[5]

Sally considers herself the least of Christ's little ones, and this book is a reflection of her little soul proclaiming the greatness of the Lord. These stories are not only reflections of Sally's spirit rejoicing in God our Savior, but also are true manifestations of how the Mighty One can do great things for all of us who aspire to believe as little children.

Our aspiration toward sanctity is never ending, and one day we will open our eyes and see why the weeds grow among the wheat. We will all, I pray, one day understand how God can reveal His glory through such concoction. This thought alone may make us restless, but we are not alone in our aspirations. Even St. Augustine knew that our hearts are restless until they rest in God[6]. Therefore, I ask you to be still, seek not so much as to be understood than to understand, read, listen, and allow our Lord to speak to you, so that you too may sing His praises, knowing that He will give you rest and has not and will not abandon you.

— Julie Artesi —
June 8, 2010

[1] St. Thomas Aquinas
[2] St. Francis of Assisi
[3] St. Therese of Lisieux
[4] St. Padre Pio
[5] Luke 10:21 (Douay-Rheims Bible)
[6] *Confessions* – St. Augustine

Foreword 2

"Everything is grace," from the lips of Saint Therese, the Little Flower, comes forth a wisdom that is undeniable. In this context, God's grace is seen as a free gift given and accepted freely by those who want to participate in God's great work of salvation for His glory and honor.

The author is one of the Lord's "little ones" who has made the mark of Jesus' cross her very own. The manifestation of the radical freedom she has exercised in her ministry speak loudly and clearly, that she has entrusted herself to the driven creative energy of the Holy Spirit. Her determination to allow that energy to flow into her, and then be released by the gifts of grace for the healing of others, is a powerful testimony of God's work within and through her.

I now recount my encounters with her. Between the years of 1993 to 1998, I, as a pastoral vicar of St. Gertrude's church in Stockton, California, was appointed by Bishop Donald Montrose as the official exorcist of deliverance ministry at the diocese. Within a short space of time, I met Sally at a prayer meeting. I recall how eager she was in helping me with the deliverance-healing ministry, in that she assisted me by praying her prophetic vision of healing into my conscious and subconscious states of mind.

An incident occurred when she asked me to bless her healing medical center. She was very thorough in describing the demons' attacks upon her and her coworkers there. Since it sounded very serious, I took with me blessed salt, blessed water, and blessed oil along with my exorcism prayers. With her guidance of these instruments of faith in Jesus and His church, her medical center was freed from demonic interference. The task was not complete until, as she insisted, every worker including herself, would have the same treatment. These prayers from the creative energy of the Holy Spirit would later form the believer of the "Precious Blood Apostolate," in which I am presently engaged in.

I have chosen one specific prayer as an illustration:

"O my Eucharistic Jesus, grant that your Holy Spirit penetrate my soul with a fiery love. Safeguard me from the attacks of the enemies of my body, soul, and spirit.
May I praise you all my days and with Mary, our beloved mother present, be your faithful, zealous apostle of spirit-filled teaching and healing ministry. Thank you for preserving me in your grace, so that I eternally sing of your mercies, given through your most precious blood. Amen."

Fr. Thomas Alkire, O. Carm.
St. Raphael Church
Los Angeles, South California

Preface

The stories you are about to read were inspired by actual events. You have been chosen, like I, to know that a merciful and Almighty Omnipotent God truly exists, and I pray that you will come to believe that His gift of grace is everlasting.

Although there was a time when I certainly did not want my life experiences made public, I remain in awe today as to how someone as lowly as I could have come to this point of publishing a book. Divine intervention is at hand, for I've always considered myself the most unwise of siblings, having had no upper-level education. During high school, I had no interest in excelling academically, no desire to expand my vocabulary, and was happily resigned to my simple lot, which accounts for why I feel, I suppose, ignorant compared to my four sisters and one brother. That's the truth of the matter, and my sisters get so angry with me when I say these things, but I feel I must disclose the truth, at least as I see it.

I think I am a bit like Moses because I grew up with a speech impediment and would get tongue-tied attempting to partake in simple conversation. As a result, my parents enrolled me in speech therapy, so I could learn how to move my tongue to enunciate properly. Yes, it was a minor setback, but this deficit did not stop me from being who I am. I mean, I am and have always been confident and joyful, and I have my sweet Jesus to thank for that. Nevertheless, as you will read in this book, the traumatizing childhood experiences did not discourage me but, on the contrary, brought me closer to Jesus; and from Him came my joy.

The thought to write this book came to me in a dream almost twenty years ago. I heard God call my name and was suddenly awestruck. Somehow I knew it was our Lord, because He spoke with a voice that emitted a resounding echo, "You will write a book and call it Everlasting Grace." A feeling of wonder and peace filled my very being, yet I dared to question, *Lord, how could I write a book?* I awakened confused—*He must know I'm no scholar*—yet I clearly knew what I must do.

For the past twenty years, I have written in notepads and journals every night or whenever I had the opportunity. Year after year, the desire to one day publish my narratives grew in intensity, and last year I realized it was time.

What you are holding is only a fraction of the full manuscript. Throughout the years, I had crossed paths with many special people and, in retrospect, never thought those same people would be a valuable asset to helping me publish this book some twenty years later. I now know that if God had not placed those people in my life, this book would still be a compilation of disjointed notes, journals, and tattered memories.

I pray that this book will inspire you to critically reflect, believe, and know that God's grace is sufficient. You must first open your heart and realize that God's ways are not man's ways, which is why I must ask you something very important: I ask that you forgive and love others unconditionally, especially those who have or continue to persecute you. Forgiveness is another word to portray how the camel passes through the eye of a needle. To put it more explicitly, forgiveness is another word for letting go of whatever keeps you from fully allowing God into your life. Chapter three recounts the story of my Aunt Sally, which manifests a special grace—the power of mutual forgiveness—the portal to God's healing power.

Chapter three also describes another time when God revealed Himself to me. He appeared as something akin to a ball of fire—an indescribable light entering my room. I know this sounds strange, but He spoke to me, not with words, as it is difficult to relay exactly, and He commanded that I lift my hands up toward heaven. He said, "I am going to bless your hands and anoint them with holy oil." It was at that moment when I realized I had received the gift of healing. Scripture speaks of such gifts, and St. Paul also warns us to beware of false angels of light. However, as you read these stories, you will know that a house divided cannot stand. Please rest assured that my testimony is true. Ever since I was a little girl, I have experienced God manifesting His presence in a variety of ways.

When I was about ten years old, I recall sitting at the dining table one bright morning watching my mother make breakfast for my father. I was sitting quietly and could see a little boy hanging on my mother's apron while she cooked. He had some of my sister Louise's facial features. I calmly asked my father, "Who is that little boy over there hanging on mom's apron?" My father replied, "What little boy? There's no one over there." He turned his head, looked at my mom in a strange manner, and repeated that he did not see a little boy. I pointed and said with agitation, "There, there's a little boy who's hanging on mom's apron!" My parents looked at each other and with a sincere and puzzled look, my father explained, "Your sister Louise," he paused, "had a twin who died at birth, but no one knows about it." He breathed deeply and added, "We've never told anyone." I was afraid. My father could see that I was afraid, so he asked me to pray for God to take away the gift of vision until I was older and able to understand such a gift. My prayer was granted, yet the gift returned decades later, as you will read. I knew God loved me but still many things occurred beyond my understanding.

As you read and reflect on chapter one, I pray you will realize that everything really does happen for a reason, and that reason is all part of God's greater plan to be unveiled in His due time.

Perhaps this little book may be God's way of reminding us that His ways are not our ways. I know that many may not believe what I am about to disclose. Nonetheless, if biblical stories did not exist, who would believe that God had summoned a murderer out of the desert to deliver His people from bondage? How could one comprehend that God had chosen someone who ordered St. Stephen's torture to instruct His Church on what is moral and just? In addition, one may wonder why Jesus knowingly left the keys to His earthly kingdom to someone who had a volatile temper and who would later adamantly deny Him. Indeed, our God is an awesome God, and He knows our hearts more than we know our hearts. He knows what we are capable of achieving and, through our obedience and supplication, He will soften the hardest of hearts just as easily as He magnifies the simplest.

— Sally Ann Quinones —

*"...all have sinned and are deprived
of the glory of God."*

— Romans 3:23 —

1

The Father's Mercy

I decided to start my first chapter telling you about a truly holy, hard working, and dedicated man—my father. He taught me how to love unconditionally; he taught me how to endure suffering without complaint or bitterness; he taught me how to live in hope. You do not have to become as old as I to look back and see with your heart that everything really does happen for a reason.

During the last years of my father's life, we were inseparable. I spent many hours with him in prayer, in thanksgiving, in laughing, and in crying. I took him to Mass, and when he became too ill to go to Mass, I brought communion to him. My father loved all of his children with an unconditional love beyond all understanding, which is why I feel it is most important to show how, through his life and death, I, rather my siblings and I, have been drawn closer to our Lord.

In 1986, my father's health declined drastically; his lungs filled with fluid, and he was hospitalized at St. Joseph's Medical

Center in Stockton, California. My father knew he was going to die, so one day while visiting him, he turned, looked at my sister Mary and said, "Take me home, that's where I want to go." Mary responded, "You know, dad, they can't take anymore fluid out of your lungs. They can't do anything else for you, dad." We then took him home, and there he remained bedridden.

It was around two o'clock in the afternoon when we brought dad home. As soon as we made him comfortable, I called Father Bill, our family priest, to come and anoint him, for we all knew our father was dying. Father Bill came right away, anointed my dad, and told our mother that if she needed him during the evening, not to hesitate to call him.

After the anointing, my dad sat up and wanted to eat, so my mother gave him something to eat. It was another miracle! The physicians told us that my father clinically died a couple of times, even though after we would lay hands on him and pray, he would wake up. These things might seem insignificant to you as a reader, but they are truly miraculous moments. He was a man who should have been dead or who certainly should not have had enough energy to open his eyes and talk. Yet he ate, talked, joked, and even played dominoes with my brother-in-law Raymond until late into the evening.

At eleven o'clock that night, I went home exhausted, did a few chores, and finally went to bed and fell asleep. Shortly thereafter, a ringing phone awakened me. It was my sister, saying, "Listen Sally, you better come. Daddy dropped into a coma, and he's not going to live through the night." I immediately called Father Bill, and he quickly came over to my parents' house.

When I arrived, I sat right next to my dad. I could see that his lips were dry and cracked, so I presumed his throat was sore and that he was thirsty. I became extremely thirsty myself and drank glass after glass of water. I must have consumed at least eight glasses. I felt as though I was drinking water for my dad, and that God was allowing me to enter into my father's suffering so I could help ease his transition into death.

I rinsed a washcloth with cool water to moisten my father's parched lips and then, suddenly, my brother stood up and moved toward my father's feet. He started to pray, and with a strong voice he said, "Father God, we thank you that you gave us a good father. Dad, you worked hard and you gave us all we needed. We thank you Lord for my father and for the faith and the trust he had in you."

Then, all at once, my father sat up with his arms outstretched as though he was reaching for someone. His eyes opened wide, and a beaming smile transformed his face from agony into joy. I knew at that moment that he was in the presence of the Lord. His arms gently came down by his side and he gently fell upon his pillow. This is the same description of how St. Bernadette died, for she too reached out, smiled, and gently fell into her eternal rest.

Upon seeing my father take his final breath, Father Bill declared, "What a death; he died in God's arms and he's with the Lord now. Louie taught his children how to live and how to die." There is certainly no doubt that Jesus will remember my dad when he comes into His kingdom.

After my father took his last breath, I tried to stand but felt numb. I really believe with all my heart that my spirit was crushed, because I was completely paralyzed. I couldn't move. I tried to walk to the bathroom but needed assistance. Rudy, my ex-husband, reluctantly helped me, but I could sense that he wanted to leave. He didn't want to be there anymore. Rudy loved my father and stayed until he passed. I couldn't have asked any more of him.

I just lost my dad, I recently lost my husband, and I felt I was losing control of my body. Someone called an ambulance to take me to the hospital, and my mother left my father's body to go along with me. My mother, a strong woman, knew daddy was with the Lord and that my brother and sisters would handle the arrangements for his body—what great saintly resilience.

The hospital assigned a psychologist and psychiatrist to evaluate me, and they diagnosed my condition as hysteria. They reassured me that my father and family loved me and were grateful for all my prayers and assistance, but I somehow knew that the Lord's hand was at work and that my condition was not a mere psychological imbalance, but a manifestation of God's great mercy. I loved my dad so very much, and the Lord allowed me to partake in my father's suffering, but why? I realize our Lord is merciful and wants us to impart mercy to those who have caused us the most suffering. I think it is through our ability to have mercy and forgive those who have hurt us the most that shows God we are truly worthy to be called His servants. After all, He sent his only Son to show us how to, "… forgive them, they know not what they do." (Luke 23:34)

We must forgive one another and never allow resentment or bitterness to enter our hearts. What I am about to disclose in the following chapter is very difficult for me to express. I thought, *Forget it, I will not say anything to cause my family shame or disrespect.* Still, I was drawn to explain how God works and how his ways are not ours. If we would only allow Him to work within our lives, He would then transform lives through our sufferings. I know our Lord wants everyone to know that love is much stronger than pain or sorrow and that no sin is greater than the love God has for each one of us. All you have to remember are the sweet words spoken by the good thief, "… Jesus, remember me when you come into your kingdom." (Luke 23:42)

"The Crucifixion" Illustrated by Pat Wilke Tadena

2

God's Transforming Grace

A s you have read in chapter one, my father died a holy death after he had spent the final twenty-three years of his life caring for those in need. His love for others and his family was genuine and unconditional; yet my father, like many fathers, was not perfect. He made mistakes and spent the remaining years of his life in atonement—what grace.

All are given the opportunity to make atonement while on Earth, but my father is one of the few who truly spent the rest of his life in reparation, not out of fear, rather out of pure desire. Our Lord truly loved my father and wanted him to remain within the fold.

As I reflect, I realize that the Lord used me as an instrument to help my father attain sanctification. Of all the chapters in this book, this one is the most difficult to articulate. Some things one cannot express effectively, but must experience them to believe.

When I was a child, I remember my father calling himself the "six-million-dollar man" before it became a TV series. To him, we were each worth a million dollars. There were six of us—five girls, and one boy. My brother was the youngest. My father's quote was, "I'm the richest poor man that ever lived." We put those words on his headstone. It reads, "The Richest Poor Man that Ever Lived."

While growing up, my father made my siblings and me walk two miles to St. Gertrude's Catholic Church to attend Sunday Mass. This routine provided his opportunity to spend quality time with my mom. We paid attention in church as best we could, because we knew that afterward, my father would reward us with a Pepsi cap if we could tell him what the sermon was about (at that time, we could get into the movies with a Pepsi cap). Our conversation time with dad was special, and he would quiz us to make sure we had listened to the priest. I knew that my father was a good man and really loved God, but that he had an alcohol addiction as well, which transformed him into an angry, out-of-control tyrant who did not know what he was doing or saying. Even as a child, I knew that the alcohol possessed him and would eventually kill him if he did not stop.

Throughout my childhood, I experienced great sorrow as well as physical and psychological pain. However, I came to see that from great sufferings I endured, glorious heavenly manifestations unveiled. I tried to stay focused on God and could never talk openly about the terrible childhood abuse I experienced. I felt it would somehow disrespect or dishonor our family. I am now choosing to share my tribulations because I do feel that it is God's will. It's time. In some strange way, grace abounds more so from a soul that has suffered much. I do not boast for my own accord. I boast only in the Lord and have come to understand that suffering is a precious gift beyond our understanding. Regardless of the sufferings I endured as a child, I always remained joyful. Somehow I knew that God was watching and caring for me.

A joyful heart is a heart that rests in the Lord, and from a joyful heart comes much laughter. Growing up, I loved to make my sisters laugh, and we had such fun playing together. At school, during class time, I would joyfully incite my friends to talk, chew gum, and be totally disruptive—but in a fun way, so I thought. Well, my ninth-grade teacher didn't think my disruptive behavior was funny. She warned me, but I didn't pay attention to her. One particular day, this behavior resulted in my getting a "blue slip," which meant she was going to call my parents. I also had to serve detention after school that day and came home very late. I knew I was in big trouble. When my dad came home that night, Mom told him what had happened at school. My father was drunk—again. My mother did not realize how drunk he was and begged, "No, don't hit her!" I knew it was too late, as I watched my father's face grow more and more angry. He looked at me and said, "Go bring me a stick so I can beat you with it! You better get a good, big stick." I thought, *If I picked a really great big stick, like a board, he certainly wouldn't be able to hit me hard with it!* So I picked up a large two-by-four and handed it to him. He took the large board from my hands; my heart raced as he lifted it up. I turned, and to my surprise, he swung down one time across my back, and that's all it took to knock me to my knees. I looked up and, even as drunk as he was, he looked surprised that he hit me with that board. He was mad at me, yes, but he was also mad at himself. He ordered me to get up and go to my room. I couldn't get up right away, but somehow I managed to crawl to the bedroom. I got up on the bed and just cried, bitterly.

Afterward, my father told my sisters not to go into the room and to leave me alone, so I could think about what I had done. I didn't know if he meant bringing in the biggest stick I could find, or getting in trouble in school. They were so worried. It is very sad and difficult to write or even talk about this experience, as almost fifty years have passed, and I have never told anyone. My father was a very good man in many ways, but he was a terror when he drank.

As a young teenager, I did not drink, smoke, take drugs, or date, so I think on the occasion when he whipped me with an extension cord, I must have otherwise annoyed him somehow. After that whipping, my sister Louise whispered to me that she wanted to help me escape and that we could both run away. She was afraid that one day daddy would really hurt me.

On that day, after my father finished whipping me with the extension cord, he again ordered me to the bedroom to stay alone. The room was dark, and the only light that came through was the light from the window. I fell to my knees to pray. Kneeling at the window, I stared up into the night sky, praying, "God if you are there, if you saw what my father did, please show me; give me a sign. That's all I need. I just need to know that you see what's happening to me." I continued to kneel, pray, and gaze out the little window at the beautiful moonlit sky, and then a fireball of light, like a meteor, suddenly appeared and struck and burned a tree branch right outside the window. It was amazing. Then I began to feel a cool, soothing, healing sensation resembling water flow against my body where the whip marks burned. Please believe me, as God is my witness, all of my pain and even the whip marks vanished!

I felt that Jesus did not want me to feel the same pain that He felt when He was scourged and hung on the cross, especially since I was just a child. I somehow felt He healed me of more than just the external scars. I did not tell anyone about the beatings, because I assumed they would think of me as only a silly thirteen-year-old. I thought, *Who would believe me?* Besides, I loved my father so much and did not want to hurt him.

It was not until five years later that I found out the extent of the injuries my father caused by striking me with the two-by-four. I was eighteen years old, married, and pregnant with my first child, Cynthia. I began experiencing severe pain in my side, and my physician ordered x-rays. After viewing the results, he asked, "When were you in a car accident?" I said, "What car accident?" He replied, "The car accident that damaged your kidney. You have a kidney that appears to have been smashed." He looked concerned and added, "It is now callused and non-functional. You must have been injured several years ago." I knew at that moment that my kidney was smashed by the two-by-four but did not want to get anyone in trouble. I said, "Well, it doesn't hurt," and smiled. The doctor looked at me a bit puzzled but then said, "People can live with one kidney, you know." He stressed, "It's dormant, it's dead, and it's callused." He then looked at me as if he knew I had suffered without medical attention and that someone had probably assaulted me. I said, "Well, as long as you don't have to take it out, and it's not bothering me, I guess I'll be alright." So we decided to leave the dead kidney alone, and I continued to pray.

Months later, I went to St. Gertrude's church and knelt before the Blessed Sacrament asking God for a miracle, not for myself but for someone else in need. As I prayed, the Lord spoke to me, "I'm going to perform a miracle on you." I said, "What kind of miracle?" He replied, "Be still, I am here." I recall that I was very quiet and still. All at once, I felt a soothing sensation like the same soothing water I had felt as a child after I had been beaten with an extension cord. The sensation flowed through me. It went right through my sides, around my kidneys, and down my lower back. I still didn't know what miracle our Lord meant to perform. I thanked Him for the soothing sensation. I said, "You know Lord, I accept whatever miracle that you just performed. I feel the healing water." I could hear the Lord's resounding voice, "I am the Living water, water, water," and a sense of peace calmed my entire being.

Three years after the Lord embraced me with His living water, I was pregnant with my third child, Jeana, and my back began to ache again. I made an appointment with my doctor and told him that when I was pregnant with my first child, my back had bothered me the same way, and I had been told I had a callused kidney. As a result, he sent me to a specialist who injected me with a certain dye to examine my kidneys. After he viewed the results, he had a strange look on his face and said, "Did you know that you have three kidneys?" I was shocked, "Three?" I asked. He said, "Yes, you have one that is callused and non-functioning, and you have another one next to it in good condition; also, you have one on the other side. At one time, you had three functioning kidneys." *Really?* I thought. He repeated, "You have two that are functioning, and the other one is no longer functioning. Did you have some kind of great fall on your back?" The moment the doctor said that at one time I had "three functioning kidneys," I reflected three years back and understood that the soothing waters I felt must have been God, the divine surgeon, giving me a new kidney.

I've come to understand that our Lord wants us to think critically. He wants us to ask the Holy Spirit for guidance. It was through the Holy Spirit that I learned God performed this miracle as an act of grace—an act to remind His human instrument that He will never abandon her. I say this boldly, because the first doctor already told me I could live with one kidney. Evidently, God gave me the third kidney to prove to the doctors and those who read these words that miracles still happen.

A definition of miracle is: "That which exceeds scientific explanation or the natural order of things." Therefore, since there is no explanation that can clarify how a kidney can suddenly appear, what we are left with is surely a miracle.

Even though my father had hurt me mentally and physically, I never stopped loving him and never stopped believing that he loved me. In some strange way, my father's cruelty taught me to love him and others more deeply than you can imagine. I was never afraid of my father; rather, I felt great sorrow for him because the alcohol took control of his senses, and he really did not know what he was doing. Even if he did, he was unable to control his actions while under the influence. No, I am not making excuses for him. I am coming to terms with his sickness.

My father truly loved me and truly loved the Lord. Yet, like most saintly men, his early years were the most trying, and the evil one was waiting with a bottle ready to devour my precious father's soul. In the end, I know our Blessed Mother struck the serpent with her heel. As a result, my father stopped drinking in 1963, and was transformed into a most compassionate, holy man. As I mentioned earlier, he spent the last twenty-three years of his life practicing corporal works of mercy.

3
Called to be Jesus' Healing Hands

"Here I am…."

"…, 'Speak, LORD, for your servant is listening.'"

(1 Samuel 3:8-9)

St. Paul tells the Church at Corinth:

There are different kinds of spiritual gifts but the same Spirit, there are different forms of service but the same Lord; there are different workings but the same God who produces all of them in everyone. To each individual the manifestation of the Spirit is given for some benefit. To one is given through the Spirit the expression of wisdom; to another the expression of knowledge according to the same Spirit; to another faith by the same Spirit; to another gifts of healing by the one Spirit. (I Cor. 12:4-9)

St. Paul wants all readers to know that each are called to serve, and he tells us that the Holy Spirit will empower us with the grace to do amazing things for the glory of God.

God revealed His glory through me in a way I could have never imagined. As you continue reading, I pray that you'll be filled with faith, hope, and love.

Gift of Healing as a Ball of Fire

One night after praying, reading the Bible for a while, and waiting for my husband, Rudy, to fall asleep, I finally went to bed. It was very late, and as I lay in bed trying to fall asleep, all at once I saw a mummy with no head. It was as if his head was unwrapped and invisible. I knew it was a male mummy, because the only body part visible was his male body part. I could see that there was thick tape around him entirely, except for this one part. His arms were stretched out, and he attempted to rape me. He got on top of me, and I screamed out, "Jesus, save me! Jesus, save me!" He fought with me, and I wouldn't let him get his way with me. I pushed him off of me, screaming, and no one heard me, not even my husband who was asleep right next to me. This mummy was holding my arms, but I kept fighting him off. Then, I screamed even louder, "In the Name of Jesus, leave!" Suddenly, this mummy, or should I say evil spirit, went right into Rudy who was fast asleep next to me. I knew that this was a spirit of lust.

After much prayer, I believe that this spirit was in Rudy and came out while he was sleeping to manifest itself and try to attack me. I asked God, "How do I get it out of here God? How do I do that?" The Lord then instructed me to look at the mattress. The mattress, where Rudy slept, had the image of a man with his arms outstretched, just as I saw the mummy when he went into Rudy. The image was on the mattress.

I immediately called a friend from the church and asked him if he would come and get the mattress out of the house, and he did. I didn't tell him what happened, but I did ask him to have the mattress burned and not to give it to anyone. I know that he did as I asked. That same day, I bought a new mattress, box spring, and new bed.

I want to get back to the evening after the spirit left me alone that night. I saw a ball of fire in the corner of my bedroom that was as big as a basketball. It was spinning fast, around and around. Then, the Lord's voice came from the ball of fire and said, "I'm very proud of you. You have just fought the enemy." Next, the ball of fire moved from the corner of my bedroom and hovered over me. Then I heard the Lord say, "Lift up your hands, so that I can anoint them." I said, "Lord, I can't, I just fought the devil." Then, unexpectedly, it felt as though angels were lifting my hands up toward this beautiful ball of fire, and warm oil fell from the ball directly onto my hands. I remember the oil feeling so warm, and I felt so blessed. This event was when I believe I received the gift of healing. God was preparing me for my healing ministry.

Aunt Sally's Healing

Do you recall reading about the time I fought the mummy in my room and received the gift of healing through the ball of fire? Well, you will see how God was preparing me at that time for the following event.

One beautiful summer evening in 1973, an evening seemingly otherwise insignificant, was the first time our Lord called me to use the gift of healing that I had received. I remember ending the day with a family Rosary and a private seven o'clock evening prayer. Later that evening, as I lay asleep in bed, God came to me in a dream. Now some may call it a vision, and those who do not believe may call it or rather, call me, deluded. However, as you may know from many scriptural stories, our Lord does speak to us in our dreams. He uses dreams to direct His people. (See Matthew 1:20.)

I heard our Lord say, "I want you to pray over Sally for seven days." Then He added that after the seven days of prayer, He would heal Sally completely. I slowly responded, "But Lord, she is dying, and the doctors said she has only two months to live. The hospital sent her home connected to a morphine drip and besides that, I don't even talk to her family. Would she even know or accept me?"

In a commanding, yet gentle voice, He replied, "Yes, now go see her every day for seven days." I hesitated not out of disobedience to God's call, but because of St. Paul's words, "...for even Satan masquerades as an angel of light." (See II Cor. 11:14.)

I then asked, "Lord, how do I know this is you?" He did not respond, so I told God, "Then, I'll ask Rudy what he thinks about me praying over his Aunt Sally."

I knew it would be a miracle for Rudy to agree that I intercede for his Aunt Sally, as his heart was full of pride and he rarely associated with his family. I quietly thought, *Well, before I speak to Rudy, I will ask for God's help,* "Lord, if I am to pray over Rudy's Aunt Sally, show me what I am to do." As quickly as I completed the sentence, I felt as if I had fallen into a dreamlike state. Yet, it felt so real.

I recall looking up and I could see a white house. The lower half of the house was brick and the upper half had two large windows on each side. I inquisitively walked toward the house and up three steps to its small porch. As I approached the entry, I noticed the screen door was worn and old. Its screen had a large tear, which flapped over a little. As I reached for the doorknob, I saw beautiful, glowing flames enveloping my hand. Although surprised, I did not feel afraid. The flames felt soothing, and I stared at their striking red and yellow luminosity gently emitting from my hands. Then I heard our Lord's voice say:

> Those are not your hands, they are my hands. Your hands become mine when you pray for the sick. I Am the Healer, and you are the vessel. Now go and pray for seven days.

After hearing the Lord's instruction, the vision dissipated.

I abruptly awoke and found I was still lying in my bed. I remember feeling very peaceful within and I said, "Lord, when I go to visit Rudy's Aunt Sally, should I pray in tongues? How should I pray?" I didn't know what to do and was afraid that if I prayed over her in tongues, it might scare her, and then she'd really think I was crazy. In a resonating voice that echoed with loving tenderness, God replied, "Pray...Our Father, Our Father, Our Father, who art in heaven, in heaven, in heaven, hallowed, hallowed, hallowed, be thy name, thy name, thy name...." His commanding yet gentle voice was beyond human description, for it resonated throughout all of my senses. Our Lord then repeated the same instructions He had given in Matthew's gospel, "You are going to heal many, and you are going to be my vessel. You must always remember that this gift was freely given to you and you are to freely give. Never take any money for the healing, because I Am the Healer." (See Matthew 10:7-8.) I promised our precious Lord in my dream that I would never take any money. To this day, I have never broken that promise.

The following morning, I told Rudy, "I want to go and pray over your Aunt Sally." He looked at me as though I were crazy—most people look at me that way, you know. Then he hesitated and said, "Sal, you know Aunt Sally is dying, why would you want to go?" Apparently, Rudy seemed to think it was pointless, so I told him about my dream. He maintained that look of disbelief, but what happened next shocked me. He agreed! "Well, go ahead and go, what can it hurt?" he replied.

I knew God stirred Rudy to submit; I just knew it, and was overjoyed. If you knew Rudy, you would understand and be overjoyed too. I waited about three days after the dream and then felt it was time to visit Aunt Sally.

On the day of my first visit to Aunt Sally, I recall it was a bright and peaceful Sunday afternoon. I just got in my car and drove out to her house. I have to say, this was all so new to me, as I didn't really know her. We had never visited or spent time together, and I was not sure how I would be received. All of this fear of the unknown caused me anxiety, but I somehow felt confident and was not about to waver. Still, during the drive to her home, my mind was filled with conflicting thoughts: *What will they think when they see me? What will they say? What will they do?* I feared, as did Rudy, that her family might very well think I'm a crazy lady. Well, I'm sure Moses felt the same way when God called him, but at least he had Aaron to speak for him. I kept driving, compelled to follow the Lord's command. I figured He must know what He's doing.

I reached Aunt Sally's home—a white house with the lower half brick. I nervously walked up the three steps to the front porch. Stunned, I stepped back a bit. My eyes fell upon the worn, old screen door, and my heart began to race. I noticed the ripped screen on the door was torn and flapped over. There it hung, exactly as it had in my dream. God had revealed this home and its details to me the week before. At that moment, I knew something miraculous, something special, was going to happen. Overwhelmed, I felt God's grace overshadow me, and for the first time, I felt what that word really meant. I felt an immense joy, confidence, and awe knowing that our Lord's healing power would manifest within this house—there was NO doubt in my mind.

I knocked. Aunt Sally's husband Bernie opened the door and smiled. He said, "Come in, I've been waiting for you." I realized at that moment that Florence, my sister Mary's neighbor, must have shared my dream with Uncle Bernie. I told him about my dream and that God had sent me. He smiled and led me to Aunt Sally's room.

I slowly walked into Aunt Sally's bedroom and saw this frail woman connected to a morphine drip and lying in a hospital bed. She was patiently awaiting death. Her tired eyes were filled with pain. Her once beautiful porcelain face was now beet red from fever. Death seemed imminent. The bone cancer was consuming every fiber of her body. Through the pain, she smiled when she saw me. I told her how our Lord spoke to me in a dream and had directed me to come and pray over her for seven days. She looked at me, and in a weak voice she whispered, "I heard. Go ahead, what can it hurt?" I remembered these were the same words Rudy said to me just the other day.

Day after day I went to Aunt Sally and prayed as the Lord commanded. However, on the third day, as I slowly recited, "Our Father who art in heaven, hallowed be thy name. Thy kingdom come. Thy will be done, on earth as it is in heaven. Give us this day our daily bread, and forgive us our trespasses, as we forgive those who trespass against us,..." Immediately, at this point in the prayer, I felt heat from my hands reflect back from Aunt Sally as if she were rejecting the healing power. I stopped praying and thought to myself, *There must be something wrong; she needs to forgive some trespass.* I softly said, "I feel that you're rejecting me. There's something wrong; because when I pray over you, I feel the healing heat returning to me. It doesn't feel quite right."

I paused, looked at her, and softly added, "What have I done to hurt you?" She seemed troubled and said, "You don't remember what you did, do you? You don't know?" I innocently responded, "No. Did I do something?" She said, "Yes. When we were pregnant together many years ago, you with your first child and I with my third, we were in the same hospital for a doctor's visit one day, and when the nurse called out 'Sally Quinones,' we both got up. You didn't give me the time of day. You didn't even look at me. You didn't say 'Oh, our names are the same, or Hi, Sally, you're Uncle Bernie's wife.' No. Nothing." She added, "You thought you were too good for us because we were poor, as if you were better than us."

I was shocked. I had no idea I had hurt her, and the thought of me thinking that I'm better than anyone else never crossed my mind. I tried to explain, "I never thought I was better than you. I was only eighteen years old, embarrassed, and scared to death that day, having my first baby. I didn't even know who you were." Still, I asked her to please forgive me for not knowing. She sighed, and we hugged. Our tears flowed, and through the sobs I said, "I would never intentionally hurt you or anyone."

Shortly afterward, I laid healing hands upon her, and this time I could feel the healing heat penetrate from my hands directly into her body.

On the fourth day, as I prayed over Aunt Sally, I had a vision of her as a child dressed in a little pink dress. She must have been only eight years old. I told her, "Aunt Sally, God gave me a vision of you standing at a corner under a stop sign. You were wearing a pink dress with flowers, and you were holding a bag in your hand." Aunt Sally started to cry. I asked, "Aunt Sally, what's the matter? What does this vision mean?" I sat next to her while she lay in bed, sobbing. She responded, "I will never forget that day. I was walking home from school and was waiting near a stop sign for someone to pick me up to take me home. My aunt, who was a nun, picked me up that day and told me that my mother had died. I felt so alone."

She stopped crying and stared at me in amazement and asked how did I know this. I stood up and said, "Aunt Sally, it was a vision that God put into my heart." She could not believe I saw an event that happened to her with such detail. I told her, "I can't wait until tomorrow to see what God is going to unveil next." She smiled, and somehow I knew she was being healed in more ways than just physically.

On the fifth day, I visited Aunt Sally and told her, "I had another vision of you. This time you were in a large monastery and sitting alone in the second pew from the front. You sat at the end of the pew against a stone wall, and your little face was staring at the altar. I saw monks and nuns around you, and I'm not sure what this vision means." Aunt Sally sat up, astonished and said, "Sally, how did you know this? Did someone tell you?" "No, tell me what?" I responded. "I know nothing about your life. I'm just describing these visions that God put in my mind, and I don't know what they mean. I don't know what God's trying to tell us."

Aunt Sally looked dazed and just stared at me, "Sally, I'm surprised you saw that. See, after my mother died, I was raised in a convent. I was placed in a convent in Irapueto with my aunt, the nun. My two brothers were sent to live in a monastery with my uncle who is a priest." She looked down, and tears flowed down her cheeks. She added, "I know what it is like to grow up and not have a mother." She looked up at me and pleaded, "Sally, I want to live. I don't want to die now and leave my children without a mother. If God would just grant me time to be with my youngest girl, Lorraine." She paused for a moment and then repeated, "Oh, if He would just grant me a little more time so I can be with Lorraine until she turns fifteen. If He would just do that for me, I would do anything God asks of me."

At that moment, little four-year-old Lorraine walked in quietly and softly said, "Is my mommy going to die?" I looked at Lorraine and then looked at Aunt Sally, who grabbed Lorraine, hugged her, and cried. I stretched my arms out and cried, "God, you have got to save her life like you told me." Later that evening, Aunt Sally said she felt renewed as if she had been bathed in warm water.

It was now day six. I continued to pray over Aunt Sally, and she said she felt different, as if something was stirring, waking up, inside. Later that day, without my knowledge, she pleaded to her husband Bernie to take her back to the hospital for another bone marrow test. She was hopeful and waited patiently for the results.

On day seven, I went to her home and noticed she was already sitting up in bed waiting for me. We prayed and thanked God. I noticed that her skin texture had improved dramatically. It was flawlessly beautiful.

About a week later, I came home from work exhausted and took a shower. I heard my children yelling and pounding on my door, "Mom, Mom, Aunt Sally's coming up our walkway. She's walking, she's walking!" I quickly came out of the shower, toweled my hair, dressed quickly, and ran to look out the window. I saw Aunt Sally walking very slowly towards my home, coming up the driveway with the help of a walker. I opened the door, and there she stood, full of life and beaming. She said, "Sally, oh Sally, I have to share something with you. We went to the hospital this morning to hear about my bone marrow results. My cancer is in remission, and even the doctors can't believe it!" She looked deeply into my eyes and said with amazement, "God did send you." I said, "Yes, Aunt Sally, God sent me."

For the next eleven years, Aunt Sally and I spent many hours attending daily Mass together. We spent time in prayer, told many about her miraculous healing, and prayed over other cancer patients. We both became more aware of how precious life is and cherished every moment as a gift. As for Aunt Sally, not one breath was taken for granted. About ten years later, in either February or March of 1983, the cancer returned. The cancer had metastasized throughout Aunt Sally's body. Her oldest daughter, Cecilia, told me that she would periodically find her mother lying prostrate on the bedroom floor in excruciating pain. Yet she was not lying on the floor from the pain, but as a sign of reverence while in deep, peaceful prayer. Cecilia added, "My mom never once complained, never felt sorry for herself."

Cecilia recalls that one night when her mother was rushed to the hospital and diagnosed with double pneumonia, the physicians called the family together and told them they were certain she would not make it through the night. Her blood pressure was dropping, and her breathing was shallow. Other family members were called in, and they rushed over to say their good-byes. Tears flowed, and the end was inevitable. Later that night, a very frail yet beautiful Aunt Sally opened her sweet Spanish eyes and managed a smile. She had no strength to lift her head between weak and gasping breaths. She whispered to her distraught daughter Cecilia, "Don't cry, Mija. I saw Jesus standing at the edge of the bed, and He told me, 'It's not your time to go yet.'"

Aunt Sally paused, and through tears she continued, "There are three things I must do before I die. First, I want to see my son, George. Second, I want to be baptized by immersion, like Jesus." Cecilia listened, and lastly Aunt Sally said, "Third, I want to see Lorraine turn fifteen." Aunt Sally survived the night, again, to the amazement of doctors and hospital staff. She slowly regained enough strength to leave the hospital yet was too weak to visit her son. Her weakness kept her housebound.

A few months later, in August 1983, Aunt Sally called her daughter Cecilia, "Mija, remember there are three things I still need to do, and I'm ready to check off number one—I'd like to see George now. Cecilia responded, "Mom, there's no way. You are too weak. You can't even walk." Aunt Sally responded, "I know I'm weak, but the Lord is going to give me the strength to see my son before I leave this world."

Cecilia obeyed. The following morning she drove to pick up her mother and was joyfully surprised to see her walking with the aid of a walker. They drove to the California State Prison in Soledad. However, when they arrived, the prison detention officer announced, "Visiting hours are over. You need to come back another time." Cecilia vividly recalls her mom's weak and trembling voice begging, "Please, sir, let me see my son, I don't have much time..." The officer cut her off and refused to hear her pleas, yet Aunt Sally continued to beg, "Officer, please. I promise I'll never come back again. Please let me see my son. I'm not going to make it much longer." Cecilia watched as her mother removed the cap from her head to reveal her bald scalp, the effects from chemotherapy, then delivered a silent final appeal to the officer. The officer looked at her and said he would check with his lieutenant. As the officer walked away, Cecilia could hear her mother's incessant prayer, "Lord, please soften his heart so I can see my son."

A few minutes later, the officer returned and led them to a visiting room where Aunt Sally was granted a visit with her son George for the last time. They spoke, they forgave, they cried. All anger, pain, and sorrow Aunt Sally begrudgingly held toward her son for so many years left her heart, and they both received inner healing that day.

According to Cecilia, the second thing her mother wanted to do before she died was to be immersed under water like Jesus. Though already baptized at birth, Aunt Sally's priest granted permission for her to be immersed under water.

In November 1983, Cecilia called me and asked if there was any church nearby where her mother could be fully immersed in water so that her wish could come true. She told me that Father gave his permission, and then I called my brother who got the thing rolling pretty fast.

My brother had some good friends who had the keys to the Four Square Church near our house and said that we could go there to baptize Aunt Sally. His friends Leonard and Pat Silvia opened the church for us and filled the baptismal font with warm water. It was in November, so it was a very cold night. I told Aunt Sally that I, too, wanted to be immersed like Jesus under water.

My brother agreed to baptize us. First, it was Aunt Sally, who after her immersion was filled with joy and ever grateful that all her prayers were being answered. Next, it was my turn, and my brother kept me under water for a while. In fact, Leonard was saying to him, "Let her up," and he finally let me up.

My thoughts were that I wanted to be with Aunt Sally and do as she did, and I also wanted my brother, Leonard, and Pat to accept me as a Christian sister. I remember they were so happy, and my brother was grinning from ear to ear. That was a special day for Aunt Sally, as her prayers were answered. I feel that God's grace was at work for Aunt Sally as well as for me that day.

Cecilia told me that her mom's third request was to see her daughter Lorraine turn fifteen. She said, "My mom somehow knew she was not going to die until after Lorraine's fifteenth birthday, November 26." Cecilia also told me that she was overjoyed to see her mother's grateful eyes filled with tears, as she watched her youngest daughter Lorraine celebrate her fifteenth birthday. Aunt Sally's third request was granted.

Three months later, Aunt Sally returned to the hospital. One day while visiting, as she lay in a semicoma, I whispered to her, "I'll be right back. I have to pick up my children from school." When I returned to the hospital an hour later, I was about to enter through the hospital doors when I suddenly felt an indescribable sensation. I stopped and felt embraced by a calm, simultaneous sense of joy and sorrow. I knew at that moment that Aunt Sally had died. That sudden sense of joy and sorrow was like a good-bye hug from her. She had been allowed to wait for me at the door, and then she departed on February 8, 1984.

Sister Maureen's Healing

A second story about God using me as a vessel to heal others involves a nun named Sister Maureen. I remember the day I met Sister Maureen. We met at a prayer group we both attended at Presentation Catholic Church in Stockton, California, and became friends. We lived in the same town as Aunt Sally. Sister Maureen had heard the testimony about my Aunt Sally's healing and came to speak with me about it. She asked me if it was possible for me to come and see her in the convent where she lived at St. Linus Catholic Church in Stockton. She said she was suffering from arthritis so bad that it kept her from doing her work. Sister Maureen loved God very much and was a dedicated servant. I made arrangements to see her at the convent. She told me, "Sally, when you come, it will take me a while to get to the door, but I'll get there. I can barely walk; the pain is so great." I said, "Okay, I will be there."

The day I went to see Sister Maureen, I arrived at her door, knocked, and waited. It took her about 20 minutes to get to the door, just as she had said. When she let me in, she told me her arthritis was so debilitating that she had to go to bed dressed in the clothes she planned to wear the next morning. She said it took her so long to get out of bed for she could hardly move until her body warmed up. She found it necessary to dress herself the night before, so she could make it to work on time in the morning. She asked me if it would be possible for me to come and pray with her on a regular basis, so I began to see her three or four times a week.

During the time I was seeing Sister Maureen and praying with her, I shared some stories of the healings that occurred at the prayer meetings I attended. By sharing other healing stories, especially with someone who is currently sick and yearning for healing, it sometimes helps them understand that God is the healer, and that He doesn't look at us as sinners but sees Jesus in each of us.

In healings, Jesus comes and touches us because of His mercy and His love. I would share some of these thoughts with Sister, and we would pray together. She knew I was there because I cared.

One particular day I visited, Sister was so happy. She said, "Sally, look at me! I can move better!" She said, "Look!" She then bent down to tie her own shoes. She could dress in pajamas at night, and no longer had to dress in the clothes she planned to wear the next day. She could feed herself at breakfast and, most important, she had been freed of the arthritis.

Shortly after I began visiting and praying with Sister Maureen, maybe one or two weeks later, she received some mail from a friend telling her about a diet that involved eating fish and taking fish oil that supposedly would improve her arthritis. She was faithful to that diet, and faithful that the Lord would heal her. I feel it was a combination of the prayers, God as the healer, and the diet that all worked together so that Sister Maureen was healed.

Happy those concerned for the lowly and poor;
when misfortune strikes, the LORD delivers them.
The LORD keeps and preserves them,
   makes them happy in the land,
and does not betray them to their enemies.
The LORD sustains them on their sickbed,
   allays the malady when they are ill.

(Psalms 41:1-4)

"… two eight-foot-tall transparent angels
came down from the sky
and stood at my doorway."

4
Encounters with Angels

"For God commands the angels
to guard you in all your ways."
(Psalms 91:11)

…"Now I know for certain that [the] Lord sent his angel
and rescued me…."
(Acts 12:11)

Many Bible scriptures narrate stories describing how angels had led, guided, warned, and protected God's people. I believe that the words of St. Basil best summarize our heavenly friends' roles: "Beside each believer stands an angel as protector and shepherd leading him to life." (See Matthew 18:10, Luke 16:22, Psalms 34:8, and Job 33:23-24.) To deny that angels exist is to deny the existence of anything God created. How could one be so bold as to say, yes, I believe in Jesus but not in what Jesus teaches? Therefore, open your eyes and know that there is a heavenly messenger watching over you as you read these words, and rest assured that he has been with you from the moment you were conceived—an utterly amazing concept—yet angels are simply a part of the natural order of heavenly beings. Please pray to our Lord and ask Him to help you set aside any underlying doubts and fears so that you may get acquainted with he who has been appointed to guard and guide you.

A Heavenly Introduction

I had the first encounter with my guardian angel one evening while driving home alone from a prayer meeting and singing, "Amazing grace, how sweet the sound that saved a wretch like me…." Suddenly, a beautiful male voice chimed in and started harmonizing with me. He sang, "…I once was lost, but now am found, was blind but now I see…." I smiled and knew it was my guardian angel keeping me company.

Now, please continue reading. Do not roll your eyes or wrinkle your nose in doubt, but know that anything is possible with God. At that moment, I decided to name my guardian angel Samuel for I considered Samuel a strong name, and I knew he had to have been big and strong because he had protected and guided me through so many dangers. Well, after I had named my angel, I wondered if God had already given him a name. So I prayed, "God, would you allow my guardian angel to tell me his name?" I spoke out loud, "Samuel, maybe that isn't your real name. If not, what is your name?" I repeated the question again, but softly, "What is your name?" I will never forget; he clearly said, "Clyde." I said, "Clyde! What kind of name is that?" Oh, I chuckled a bit as you probably are, and

I thought, *I don't want to tell anyone my angel's name is Clyde.*
I was embarrassed. Clyde did not sound like a strong, fierce
name, so I refused to call him Clyde. I still called him Samuel.

One day, while at a friend's home, she showed me a book
of names and their meanings. I asked her to look up "Clyde."
She said, "Hmm, here it is. Clyde means STRENGTH." As
she read, my eyes opened wide, for I was surprised and remember
falling to my knees praying, "Clyde, I will never call you
Samuel again. I like your name—Strength. You have been my
strength. You have kept me safe and have helped me stay on
the right path. Oh, Clyde, please help me while I'm here on
earth so I can reach Heaven one day." I know that I am still
alive today because Clyde, together with our Lord, has been
watching over me.

A Crash and Unexpected Intervention

One ominous rainy day, my daughter Jeana and her one-year-
old daughter and I were travelling on the freeway, when suddenly a car cut us off causing us to swerve and hit a concrete
embankment. We heard the car hit the wall and heard the
metal bending and crunching upon impact. Its force jerked us
uncontrollably inside the car. In seconds, we knew the damage
was extensive. However, I was too concerned with my wailing
one-year-old granddaughter strapped in her car seat in the back
of the car to react.

Next, out of nowhere, a big, tall, strong man appeared
and tapped on our window asking, "Is the baby okay?" I said,

"Yes, she's okay." He said, "Take your car to get it checked. Make sure they check your brakes." I said, "Okay." Jeana and I then stepped out of the car to look at the damage. The car's body was fully intact—not a scratch—unbelievable. We immediately turned to look for the stranger, and he was gone—nowhere to be found or seen. We were on the freeway when all of this happened within seconds. There was no way the man could have walked or run out of sight that quickly. We knew it was Clyde—my guardian angel who chose to reveal himself as a tall, strong man.

I enjoy talking about Clyde and think he is happy to hear me talk about him, because he wants all of us to know that our guardian angels have been neglected far too long. Oh, if only we knew how much they are allowed to care for us, we would be as little children looking forward to another day with one who sees the face of God.

Angels Ward Off Danger

Late one cold Halloween evening in 1976, shortly after nine o'clock, I had just turned off the lights after passing out candy to the neighborhood children. I did not have any candy left; I was alone; and began closing the drapes when the doorbell rang. I thought, *God, it can't be more kids at this late hour!* I opened the front door and suddenly realized that I had forgotten to lock my wrought iron security door. There on my doorstep stood a large man with dark piercing eyes that did not seem to blink, and in a deep menacing voice he said, "I need to use your phone because I ran out of gas." I immediately sensed I was in danger. I looked at him and then looked down and noticed he had placed his foot in the doorway to block me from closing the door. He looked right past me into my home and stared at my altar. It was a small altar, which held holy pictures and a prayer candle. The stranger's face became hardened as if some evil took control of him, and in a threatening voice he shouted, "I need to use your phone now!" I do not have a threatening voice but I spoke up in a trembling voice and said, "My husband is right around the corner. He's on his way home. If you look over there, you'll see him coming."

I was scared and silently prayed over and over, *Jesus, I need your help. Jesus, I need your help.* Somehow I knew this man had hurt others before and was planning to rob, rape, or even kill me. Just as he was about to charge into my home, two eight-foot-tall transparent angels came down from the sky and stood at my doorway. One stood to my right in an upright position like a soldier with a sword and bearing a stern face, and the other angel placed himself behind me, and I could see he wrapped his arms around me in protection. The man's facial expression suddenly changed into one of shock and fear. He seemed to tremble and stepped backwards with his mouth hanging wide open and his eyes wide open and filled with fear. He turned from my doorway and jumped over things I had stacked on my front porch and ran as fast as he could to his car. I noticed there were three other men in the car as they all sped away.

I have always known that our God is an awesome God, and many years after this incident I picked up the Bible and read this scripture:

> God will rescue you from the fowler's snare...
> Will shelter you with pinions,
> spread wings that you may take refuge;
> God's faithfulness is a protecting shield.
> You shall not fear the terror of the night....
> (Psalms 91:3-5)

There is no doubt that our Lord sent His angels to help me, and I will always trust "The Angel who has delivered me from all harm...." (Genesis 48:16)

I Do Not Walk Alone

In 1994, I moved back to California. I lived in a nice little condo. The complex didn't have a gym, so I would go outside early each morning about five o'clock to walk. Because the community was gated, I had to use a remote to open the gate. Being new to the area, I'd occasionally walk to the store, turn around, and come back home. The entire walk was about three miles. Heading back home from the store, on one side of the road was the freeway with nothing else but trees and brush. On the other side were condos and apartment houses. The area was quite isolated, so if someone were screaming, nobody else would be able to hear them.

On the fourth morning, while on my way home, I was walking along when I noticed a car turn the corner and then drive toward me. It suddenly stopped, and the headlights went out. Although the car was somewhat of a distance away, it was close enough for the driver to see me through dawning sunlight. I felt uneasy, and a sense of foreboding danger caused my heart to race. I thought, *Oh, God, what do I do? Do I keep walking? What do I do, Lord?* Fear was quickly covering me like a net of anguish, but I kept walking closer and closer toward the vehicle. I kept praying, for I was now only several yards from the car and I knew the driver could see me clearly.

As I wanted to quickly walk past the car, I could see that the driver was a man. My thoughts were that he was watching me come closer and closer. He then turned on the car's inside lights. It seemed obvious to me that he wanted me to see him and to know that he was waiting for me. My heart raced faster. My breathing increased. *What is he going to do? Is he waiting for me? Do I get on the other side? Do I stay where I am?* He was on the other side of the road, but when he saw that I was coming closer to him, about ten feet away, he made a u-turn. Although still a little distance away, I could see him, and he could see me.

I kept walking, slowly. I took my black, square-shaped remote out of my pocket and put it next to my ear pretending I had a cell phone. This tactic did not bother him; he continued stalking me.

As I continued to walk, I came closer to his car and thought, *Clyde, do you see that man over there? He's waiting for me. I'm scared. What do I do?* I was afraid to go across the street, thinking the man might make another u-turn. In faith, I said, "Clyde, can you show yourself to this man? Just walk beside me, so he can see you." Then I said, "God, please help me. This man is up to no good."

All at once, the man started his car and took off in a manner that suggested he had seen something that changed his mind about bothering me. He immediately raced around the corner at high speed—his tires screeching. I didn't see Clyde, but I believe that man did. I thanked God and Clyde for saving me from all harm that day. I will certainly not tempt our Lord, but have learned it is not wise to venture out alone.

A Special Christmas Tree

Another experience I had with Clyde took place one Christmas. I remember I bought a great big Christmas tree that year. My daughter told me, "Mom, don't try to put up that tree by yourself because you're going to need help. It's very heavy." I said, "I know, I'll wait." On the other hand, I've never prided myself in having much patience, and when I want something done, I want it done now!

The new Christmas tree was a large artificial one, packed in a big box. I thought about the challenge ahead and said to myself, "I can do this." Dismissing the conversation I had with my daughter, I pulled the tree out of the box and started putting it together. The tree was in three pieces. The first two I put together myself. Things were progressing nicely—until

I attempted to put the top section onto the bottom two. You see, I'm a short lady. Although I had a ladder, I couldn't pick up the heavy treetop from the floor while standing on the ladder. I continued to struggle to get that tree up but just couldn't manage. There was no way I could do it alone. I placed the top of the tree close to the ladder again and remember saying, "Clyde, I need your help. You grab one side of the tree, and I will grab the other. Together we'll get this tree set up. I want to decorate it today and get it all set for Christmas. That's my plan. Will you help me?" Once again, I tightly grasped the treetop and proceeded to lift it up and, honestly, it seemed as if someone was lifting it up with me. It was light! In amazement, I raised it higher and placed it in the hole on top of the middle piece. There it was. I got the tree up—Clyde and I, that is. Oh, and it was a beautiful tree. I said, "Thank you, Clyde. You've come to my aid again. I know you're here with me."

Clyde can hear me, and so can your guardian angel. I believe that your guardian angel is with you, can hear you, and can help you. Have you ever heard stories of people picking up heavy things that they never should have picked up? In life and death situations, others have done it. I did it. People wonder and ask how could we ever have done it. Some say it's an inner strength that takes over. I say, no, it's your guardian angel. It's that angel that God has given you for all of your life. Your guardian angel is with you from the time of birth until you die. I don't know what happens to him after that. I just don't know—but I will find out when I die.

"The Holy Eucharist"
Illustrated by Pat Wilke Tadena

5
The Reality of the Eucharist

Sometimes our Lord uses little children to help lead us closer to Him. It is through these little ones that we, the most sinful and sorrowful, humbly fall to our knees like St. Thomas, the scales removed—and it is only then when we can respond with childlike faith.

In 1973, prompted by a child, I was granted the gift of humility. While teaching Catholic Christian Doctrine, CCD, to a group of curious and skeptical sixth-grade children, a few lively boys challenged me. One persistently inquired, "Sally, I don't believe Jesus is in the Eucharist. How could He be in the Eucharist? Jesus was a man, He died, He's in heaven, and now you expect us to believe He's in the Eucharist?" He watched my reaction as the other boys eagerly watched and listened. He then added, "Yeah, hey, how can Jesus be all over the world at the same time in every church and all the tabernacles? How can He do that?" I'm sure I looked a bit shocked having taken for granted that Jesus is in the Eucharist, and that's it. I responded appropriately, however, as would any good CCD teacher. I remember looking at him and saying, "Okay, well, I don't have an answer for you right now, but I will do my best to find one. And when I do get the answer, I am going to tell you." These skeptical boys raised their eyebrows, and I was sure they wondered why I didn't have a ready answer.

This situation bothered me. I was concerned that my lack of understanding our core belief only added to their disbelief. After class, I just sat there and thought about what the young man had said. *How could Jesus be in the Eucharist? Oh no—I never thought about how; I just know that He is...right? Is He?* I began to doubt. Underneath all my scriptural study, I realized I was just as skeptical as the children. I felt a bit anxious and pondered how I could teach this sacrament. I went to Father Armand and confessed, "I don't know if I can teach sixth-grade CCD anymore...," and I informed him what had happened in class. Father Armand said, "Sally, ask God for the gift of faith. Ask him for the gift of faith, because it takes faith to believe that Jesus is in the Eucharist."

Every morning at six o'clock, Father Armand and Father Gordon gathered and prayed their Holy Hour and invited me to join them. We prayed for God to grant me the gift of faith, and I pleaded to God that He might reveal Himself to me. I became zealous. I had to know. I had to feel. I had to believe with no doubt or reservation that Jesus is truly present in the Eucharist. I thought, *Is that what He meant when He said, "I will be with you always?"* I only became more restless.

I took Father Armand's advice and joined him in daily Holy Hour for six months. Yes, every day for six months I went to church to pray at six o'clock in the morning, and afterward returned home to wake up my children and send them off to school. I then rushed back to church to complete my prayers. During this time, I was unaware that my sister Mary had asked a friend of the family, Monsignor DeGroot, to invite me to attend a Cursillo—a Catholic retreat, which originated in Spain.

Late one evening, the doorbell rang unexpectedly, and there stood Monsignor DeGroot wearing his usual magnetic and most beautiful smile, "Oh Sally, I've been trying to reach you for ten years, I want to invite you to attend the next Cursillo." At first, I gave him many valid excuses why I could not possibly attend at this time. I had too many obligations, too many chores, and too many tamales to prepare, but somehow all the obstacles I presented were resolved—easily. The next thing I knew I was in a van heading for the retreat center.

On the first retreat day, I smiled, walked in with Bible in hand, held my head high, and felt confident and ready to share my scriptural knowledge. I was ready to raise my hands high in praise and ready to lead people to Christ. On day two, after listening to the speakers, I became a little uncomfortable. I learned a very basic Christian principle—the Word of God is to be lived. I was to live it. I was to become the Word—the living Gospel. I was taken back at this new way of seeing and thinking, because I truly thought God had called me to attend the retreat so that I could use my scriptural knowledge to teach others. I suppose you can say I thought it was all about me. I was disappointed and greatly humbled. I suffered from *spiritual pride.* I remember the look of concern in Monsignor DeGroot's eyes as he pulled me aside, "Sally, you are now in a Cursillo retreat. This is not a charismatic session, so I don't want you praying in tongues, and please do not lift your arms in praise. There are a lot of people here who have never prayed out loud. I know you're very open to the Holy Spirit, but please follow direction." I humbly responded, "Okay Father." I was hurt and began to resent. I thought, *Fine, I'll shut up now. What did I come here for? They're telling me I can't talk; I can't raise my hands! I can't believe it—me?* I remained quiet, but I listened.

We were now in the third day of the retreat, and a very nice priest arrived to speak about the central facet, the heart of the Catholic faith—the Eucharist. He began with a little story about a man named Joe.

Joe was a kind and spiritual man, known and loved by many. He spent twenty-five years as caretaker for a certain church. Before starting work, each day Joe would kneel before the Blessed Sacrament and say, "Good morning, Jesus. This is Joe. I want you to know that I love you." Tragically, one day while on his way to church, a car struck Joe as he crossed the street. A young lady witnessed the horrible accident and quickly ran to the priest's home, shouting, "Father! Father! Please come quick. It's Joe! He's been hit by a car!" As soon as Father heard that a car had struck Joe, he grabbed the pyx containing the Eucharist and ran to him. Father opened the pyx and heard a voice come from the Eucharist, "Joe, this is Jesus. I just want you to know I love you." Father gave Joe communion, and then Joe died." I sat quietly. I listened intently and thought, *Now, isn't this something? Now they got the communion talking.* Obviously, my faith, even after six months of daily prayer, was still half the size of a mustard seed. I knew that if I could not fully believe in the real presence of Jesus in the Eucharist, I would have to discontinue teaching. The story of Joe did not increase my faith.

After Father finished the story, he asked each of us in the room, "What did you get out of the talk? What do you think the Eucharist is Sally?" And out of my mouth came a response I wasn't expecting, "Oh, the Eucharist is like the sun. Without it, you can't grow." I thought, *Where did that response come from? I don't even believe in the real presence, so why did I say that?* It must have been the Holy Spirit speaking through me.

Later that evening when I went to bed, I kept saying to Jesus, "That was you. You're like the sun. The Eucharist is like the sun. Without it, we can't grow."

The morning sun crept through my window. It was now the last day of the retreat, and still I was unsettled as to how I felt or if my faith had increased. I had not been to confession in more than eighteen years, and I didn't feel the need to consult with a priest just because I didn't believe Jesus was in the Eucharist. As I was kneeling in the chapel before the Blessed Sacrament, Monsignor DeGroot walked in and stood next to me. Instantly, I saw a blazing light come through the window and hit the tabernacle. I could feel heat coming from the tabernacle and coming toward me. I looked up at the crucifix. Then I sensed a metallic taste in my mouth, so I wiped my mouth with my hand and saw that it was blood. I kept looking at the crucifix and almost shouted, "You *are* in the Eucharist!" The minute I acknowledged that Jesus is in the Eucharist, the blood flow in my mouth stopped, although I could still feel its warmth. In awe, I turned to tell Monsignor DeGroot, "Father, I see! Jesus IS in the Eucharist!"

When I looked at where the Monsignor had stood, I saw Jesus kneeling next to me. He said, "Beyond the priest, I am. Come, humble yourself. It is I who forgives your sins." I instantly knew His voice and immediately understood the meaning of the Sacrament of Confession and why it was necessary. My eyes drooped; my body grew limp; and I fainted. When I awakened, I immediately confessed to Monsignor.

My confession lasted more than two hours. He cried when I looked at him and said, "Oh, Monsignor, who am I to say I don't need a priest, when you've given up your whole family and everything to help others come closer to God? I remember asking him to forgive me for being so arrogant in thinking I did not need a priest and that I did not need to go to confession—again he wept.

I was humbled, and mere words cannot express the deep faith and conviction this experience imparted. Monsignor James DeGroot went to be with the Lord on October 15, 1982. I thank God for the amazing grace and humbling experience of using me as an instrument to remind Monsignor that he was Christ, *in persona Cristi,* and that God has not forgotten those who leave mother, father, sister, or brother for His sake, for they shall receive their heavenly reward.

After some critical self-reflection, I could trace the pattern of God's work. He inspired my young student to question His presence in the Eucharist. This question inspired me to seek resolution. My six months of supplication for faith moved my sister Mary, Monsignor DeGroot, and many others to clear the path for my stay at the Cursillo retreat. At the Cursillo, I heard the story of Brother Joe, which inspired me to enter the chapel to pray, unaware that Monsignor would be entering the chapel shortly thereafter.

These events were all a part of our Lord's divine plan. My venture toward the truth was a time of great trial, and as I iterate these words, I feel Monsignor wept because he may have been experiencing a trial of his own.

After leaving my Cursillo and experiencing the true presence of the Eucharist, I started going to daily Mass. One day, at least a year later, while Father Gordon was consecrating the bread and wine, I saw Jesus transformed right before my eyes in the Host. I saw the risen Christ, just as the scripture, Matthew 17:2, describes: "And he was transfigured before them; his face shone like the sun and his clothes became white as light." This scripture best describes how I saw Jesus in the Eucharist that day. I also heard God's voice say to me, "This is my beloved Son. Follow Him, and He will lead you to the kingdom."

I later shared this testimony at Wednesday prayer meetings I led with Father Tom at St. Gertrude Catholic Church, and also with the artist who depicted this vision in a drawing, now framed and displayed in my home.

Twenty-two years after I experienced this personal revelation of the Eucharist, Father Tom Alkire asked me to share my testimony with some RCIA participants. RCIA, Rite of Christian Initiation of Adults, is a faith journey for those wishing to join the Catholic Church. I couldn't tell Father no, but I also wondered who would believe me.

The morning I was scheduled to speak, I woke up at five o'clock and prayed. I asked the Lord for some words, so that the RCIA group would believe me when I spoke to them about the real presence in the Eucharist. Then I heard these words come to me, and I wrote them down. The words formed into a poem. I feel that I was inspired by the Holy Spirit on March 30, 1996. I now have this poem framed and displayed in my home.

❧

Bread from Heaven

I am the bread from heaven,
food for the journey of faith.
I came to give you life
and fill you with my grace.
I am the bread from heaven,
sent so you may eat
my Father's way,
that you become one with me.
I am the bread from heaven
waiting to be known
as your Lord and Savior,
the one who was scorned.
I am the bread from heaven
healing, touching, sharing.
You're always in my sight.
I am who I am.
I am the bread of life.

*"My spirit left my body in a matter of seconds,
and I found myself standing in heaven."*

6
Spiritual Battle

When we're doing God's work, I'd like to emphasize that it seems obstacles are thrown our way from the enemy, designed to prevent us from doing that work.

Hit by a Ram in the Chest

At the time of this event, I was attending Wednesday night prayer meetings at my home parish, St. Gertrude Catholic Church in Stockton, California. Father Tom and I were the prayer leaders, and part of our prayer time included deliverance-healing. During this time, we prayed over people for healing of various ailments, such as illness or depression.

One night, a lady asked me for healing prayers. Father Tom was with me, and as I prayed over her, I suddenly felt a physical jolt, as if something hit my chest so hard it knocked the wind out of me. I grabbed onto the altar to steady myself, otherwise I would have hit the floor. I could not breathe and had to sit down in the pew because I felt like I was going to faint and wondered if I'd had a heart attack. Then I realized that a spiritual battle was going on, because it felt as if something evil came out from this woman and attacked me. Pete, a prayerful man on the team who had the gift of vision from the Holy Spirit, said, "Sally, I saw a ram coming full force at you." I thought, *How did he know?* That's literally what it felt like. Father Tom immediately prayed over me, commanding the spirit to be gone in the name of Jesus.

I had experienced spiritual attacks at home or while alone in the car on occasion, but never at a prayer meeting with so many people around me. This was the first, and last, time such an incident has occurred.

I want to explain to you that the woman who needed prayer that night was not possessed. Somehow a spirit had attached itself to her and oppressed her own spirit. It made her sick, unable to sleep, and depressed, and she had no idea what was causing these issues. I, too, have no idea why it had attached itself to her. Sometimes this can happen from lack of prayer, proximity to depressed and negative people, addictions, not practicing one's faith, and in the case of Catholics, not attending Mass and not receiving the Eucharist. There are evil spirits in the world that are just waiting to attach themselves to a weak-spirited person. In the scriptures, Ephesians 6:10-11, we read:

> Finally, draw your strength from the Lord and from his mighty power. Put on the armor of God so that you may be able to stand firm against the tactics of the devil.

Seeing the Lamb of God Who Filled Me with Energy

That same night, after I went home, I said my prayers and turned over to go to sleep. While thinking about being hit by the ram at the prayer meeting, I had a vision.

My spirit left my body in a matter of seconds, and I found myself standing in heaven. I saw a gate where Jesus was standing just inside. At St. Gertrude's church, in the chapel, over the tabernacle is a stained glass window with an inscription, The Lamb of God. That is the way I saw Jesus in this vision, as the The Lamb of God who takes away the sins of the world. Jesus had a lamb next to him with His shepherd's staff in hand. I went through the gate, and I stood before Him and said, "You are the lamb of God who takes away the sins of the world." and then I was back in my body. He filled me with grace.

The next day, I called Father Tom and told him about my vision. He said, "Sally, that's a grace. God filled you because you got knocked hard last night during spiritual warfare."

I want to share with you that God's grace is for everyone. You only have to ask and then you will receive. I believe if we ask the Lord in prayer and wait for His answer, He will answer.

St. Paul recalls our Lord's words in II Corinthians 12:9, which reads:

> …'My grace is sufficient for you, for power is made perfect in weakness.' I will rather boast most gladly of my weaknesses, in order that the power of Christ may dwell with me.

*"We know that all things work for good
for those who love God,
who are called according to his purpose."*

— Romans 8:28 —

7
Extraordinary Experiences

The following stories reveal God's everlasting grace in action as a result of prayer. The miraculous encounters experienced by me and other family members are a true testimony that our Lord is alive and well today—the same yesterday, today, and tomorrow.

Premonition of My Mother's Serious Illness
One evening I was lying on the couch at home. I wasn't feeling very good that night as I recall. I thought that if I prayed the Rosary I would feel better, but that didn't happen. The comfort I've received in my life when praying the Rosary is why I continue to pray the Rosary. When I need something or need to hear God's direction, or if I need an answer, I get on my knees and pray my Rosary. I'm telling you; an answer comes that quick. Well, that evening I was praying my Rosary while lying on the couch, and my mother kept calling me and saying, "I don't feel good, Sally." I responded, "Neither do I, mom."

She said she was having a difficult time breathing, but I said, "Mom, let me call you back. I need to lie down for a little bit." Then she told me she really didn't feel good and that she was starting to get scared. I said, "Mom, you need to go get some water and call me a little later." I was feeling bad myself and told her, "You're getting yourself hysterical over worry, mom, and that's why you can't breathe."

I went to lie down again but realized that I, too, couldn't breathe. I felt as though I was sharing my mom's pain. I then started praying the Rosary, and suddenly I had a vision. I saw a hospital bed, an ambulance gurney, and actually somebody covered with a white sheet lying in the gurney. I looked closer to see the person's head. It was my mother. I also saw the Blessed Mother standing next to the gurney. Next, I saw a room number; it was 332.

This vision upset me, and I felt I needed to get up and go to my mother. Hastily, I went and picked her up and took her to the emergency room at St. Joseph's Medical Center in Stockton. Tests indicated she had blood clots in both lungs. From the ER, they transferred her to a regular hospital room. It was the same room I had seen in my vision—room 332.

The next day, I bought a statue of the Blessed Mother at the hospital gift shop. Amazingly, the statue looked exactly the way I had seen the Blessed Mother in the vision.

My mother was a heavy smoker at the time of this incident. The doctors treated the blood clots with Coumadin through an IV. The clots soon dissolved, and she was healed. After a week, she returned home, placed the statue in her front room, and kept it there always.

After my mother died, however, all of her things were picked up or put away, so I don't know what happened to the statue. I believe the Blessed Mother interceded for my mother on the day I had the vision. God and His grace allowed me to share in my mother's pain, and He gave me that vision so that I could attend to her needs. Ephesians 2:8-10 says:

> For by grace you have been saved through faith, and this is not from you; it is the gift of God; it is not from works, so no one may boast. For we are his handiwork, that God has prepared in advance, that we should live in them.

Another Vision of My Mother's Health

Another time I was praying, I had a vision of my mother who was sitting in a great big chair. She was dressed in white with a Bible in her hand. Her hair was quite long, and she looked very young. She looked absolutely beautiful. She said to me, "Sally, pray for me."

I remember the next day I asked my sister Mary, "Do you think mom could be sick? I had a vision last night about her." My sister answered, "Well, let's take her to the doctor and find out."

After my mother went through some tests, the doctors told us she had cervical cancer. They operated and saved her life. You see how God works? This is everlasting grace in action.

Psalms 32:8 says,

"I will instruct you and show you the way you should walk,
give you counsel and watch over you."

Auditory Bilocation about My Father

One time while walking down an aisle picking up groceries in the grocery store, I heard my father's voice call me. It was so clear, as though he were in the store too. I heard him say, "Sally!" I looked around and thought to myself, *Is my father in here?* I heard his voice again call me, "Sally, help me!"

I left my groceries in the cart and went directly to my parent's home. My father was having a heart attack. He was slumped in a chair. I called the ambulance, and they came right away.

There it was again, God's grace, which allowed me to hear my father's voice, even though he was nowhere near me. This spiritual intervention saved my father's life. He stayed in the hospital for about a week until the doctors saw that he was much better. With instructions for a good diet and his medication, he went home. My father was extremely happy that I heard his call.

Again, God's everlasting grace was working through me. "So let us confidently approach the throne of grace to receive mercy and to find grace for timely help." (Hebrews 4:16)

Out-of-Body Experience

Another spiritual intervention happened when my sister's best friend Joanne had cancer. One night, my spirit left my body. That's a grace in itself. I've never asked for this to happen to me; it just happens, and I never know when it's going to happen. Well, Joanne was dying in the hospital in San Jose, and I remember my spirit traveled to her bedside. I prayed with her. She saw me and said, "Sally, will you please tell your sister Louise to come see me? I don't have long, and I want to see her before I go." Directly afterward, I remember going back into my body.

Early the next morning, I called my sister Louise and told her what happened. I've always shared my experiences with my sisters, Mary and Louise, since we were very young. Other people would think I am nuts, but my family knows that I'm not. They know these testimonies are true.

Louise immediately flew to San Jose to visit her friend. I had described to her the hospital room I saw in my "visit," as well as what Joanne was wearing and how she looked. My sister remarked, "Sally, you were there! When I got to the hospital room, it was just as you described!

A few days after my sister's visit, her friend Joanne died. They were very good friends. Joanne loved Louise, and Louise loved Joanne very much, as they had been best friends since high school. Louise was so happy and grateful that she was able to see her friend before she left this earth. II Corinthians 12:3 states, "And I know that this person (whether in the body or out of the body I do not know, God knows) was caught up into Paradise and heard ineffable things, which no one may utter."

Freddy's Death

When I lived in Florida, my children's Uncle Freddy, their father's brother, was dying in San Francisco. I remember one night I was in bed and I heard Freddy calling me, "Sally, Sally." It was his voice, and he said, "Sally, call me!" I thought, *He wants me to call him? I don't even know his number. I haven't seen him in years.* Again I heard him call me, "Sally, Sally," so I got up and called my daughter. I said to her, "I know it's late and I'm sorry I'm calling, but I need Uncle Freddy's phone number." There was a three-hour time difference between Florida and California. My daughter told me not to call Freddy because he was very sick. She said, "He's dying, mom." I said, "I know, but I have to call him."

The next day, I called Freddy. He answered the phone, and I said, "Freddy, it's Sally." He replied, "Thank you so much for calling me. Sally, I've been waiting for you to call me so I can tell you I love you, and that I've always loved you."

Freddy worked at the San Francisco UC Hospital. He also landscaped as a hobby because he was gifted at making yards so beautiful. He just loved to do it. He told me he had hoped to come and do my yard, but then he got real sick in 1992 and couldn't do it. I told him that I heard he was very sick and that it was okay that he wasn't able to do it. I asked him, "You're not afraid, are you Freddy?" He said, "Yes, Sally, I was very afraid. But you know what happened?" And I said, "No, what happened, Freddy?" He said, "Well, my cousin David came to visit me." (David had died years before, on July 26, 1981.) He repeated, "David came to me." Then I said, "He did? What did he say?" "Cousin David said that before I die, I need to forgive everybody who ever hurt me, and I need to forgive them from my heart. Then he said he would come and get me, and I would go where he is. He said so. I'm not afraid Sally, because I know I'm going to go with David." I said, "Oh, really, that's wonderful he came to see you." Freddy said, "Yeah, he looked good. He told me not to be afraid, but he said I must forgive everybody from my heart." Then Freddy said to me, "If I've ever hurt you, I want you to forgive me." I answered, "Oh, Freddy, you have never hurt me. Please don't think that you have, because I have never been mad at you for anything."

When Freddy died on February 13, 1992, I shared that story with family members. Freddy was cremated, so they opened David's grave and burried Freddy's ashes with his cousin. I thought that was a wonderful thing that they could be together.

I believe that David came to visit Freddy. David didn't come with any anger or anything to hurt Freddy. He came to tell him to forgive others with his whole heart. He told him that after he's forgiven everybody who's ever hurt him, that he would come for him and take him to be with him. So Freddy wasn't afraid to die after that. He said, "I am not afraid anymore. I don't know where I'm going, but I know I will be with David." That's just a wonderful thing that God allowed David to go visit his cousin so that he wouldn't be afraid, and so he could prepare himself for death.

God, in his love, sends a familiar face, so we won't be afraid of the unknown. I also believe with all my heart that when we die, it's not death, it's new life.

John 3:16 says:

> For God so loved the world that he gave his only Son, so that everyone who believes in him might not perish but might have eternal life.

Uncle Vincent and Grandfather's Visit

I believe that even after we die, we go on and live in eternity, just like it says in the Bible. After we die, though, we live in a spiritual realm. God has different things for us to do, and it always starts with our family. I believe that unfinished business can still get finished even after death.

My family has a long history of affliction from Alzheimer's. We have had seven family members die from this hereditary disease. The men in our family seem to get it more often, and typically they die before age fifty. My Uncle Vincent and his son both died from it. My mother's father, Juan Hernandez, also died from the disease.

Having Alzheimer's in the family was a source of shame for some reason, and our mother always told us that my grandfather had died from barbed wire fencing going through his head from a car accident. However, he died in 1920 in the state hospital in Stockton, California, from Alzheimer's. My mother didn't want anyone to know her father died in the state hospital for fear they would think he, or the family, was crazy.

This story is unbelievable. It's an example of why I feel that we live on in a spiritual realm after death, and that we are still alive in Christ. I believe that's what the Communion of Saints is all about.

━━━━━━━━━━━━━━ ❧ ━━━━━━━━━━━━━━

When I was married, my Uncle Vince started showing signs of Alzheimer's. My Aunt Luz didn't know what to do. Uncle Vince was only in his forties when he started displaying symptoms. He would forget the littlest things. These changes were unusual for him, because he was so smart—almost a genius. He was a very knowledgeable man and, at that time, he was a policeman with the State Department. My Aunt Luz used to bring him to visit my parents, and I would see him then too. I was about twenty at the time and had a home of my own nearby.

One day Uncle Vince was sitting and not saying too much. The disease was already getting to him, but doctors had not yet diagnosed him with Alzheimer's. No one knew for sure what was wrong with him. I kept seeing a double person in Uncle Vince. I looked into his face and could see him as he was in the physical world, but I could also see his spirit coming and going from within his eyes. I thought I was seeing things, but I didn't say anything to anyone about this. Every time he would visit my parent's house, I didn't like to sit near him because I would see that change take place in his face.

At home one night, after I said my prayers and fell asleep, I had a vision that woke me. I saw a light in a doorway, and near it stood a man. I wasn't afraid because somehow I knew within me that it was somebody that God had sent. I think God gives you a special grace when He's going to do something special.

I saw a man wearing khaki pants, a khaki shirt, a safari hat, and boots. He just looked at me. He was a small man of Spanish descent. I realized then I was seeing a vision of my deceased grandfather. I had never met him, as he had died before

I was born. I recognized him, however, from a photograph my mother had in her front room when I was growing up. This man in my vision had a mustache like my grandfather's, just as I remembered from the picture. Through his eyes he spoke to me and said, "In the morning, I want you to go on a visit to the state hospital. Once you are there, you will receive information so you can help my son Vincent." I didn't say anything in response but went back to sleep, and the vision went away.

In the morning, I got up and got myself ready. I got in the car and headed to the state hospital. I saw a vision of my grandfather again, this time through the rearview mirror. He was sitting in the back seat of my car. I arrived at the state hospital and went to the office. The woman there was helpful and kind. I explained that I was there because my grandfather, Juan Hernandez, had died there. I asked her if she had any information about his death. I only knew the story my mother told me, that he had died because of a car accident, and that the accident had caused barbed wire to go through his head.

I asked her, "What is your name?" She replied, "Lydia." I asked, "Can you look up his record and see if you can find any information about him?" Because of privacy laws, Lydia told me she could not give me the information, but she said she could give me his file number. She wrote down the file number for me and said, "Your mother or another direct relative can take this number to the courthouse, and they will give you a document to allow his papers to be released to your family. Then you can read his whole file and find out the details of his death."

Strange as it seems, this event of my going to the state hospital took place because my grandfather appeared to me and told me to go there. It was God's grace working in my life. My sister Mary is the only person who ever believed me when all of these inspired events took place, so I went to see her. I knew I could tell her about it, and she wouldn't laugh at me. She responded, "Let's go check it out."

My sister wanted to go back to the hospital first to confirm the instructions from Lydia. She wanted to speak with Lydia to find out why our mother was the only one who could get the court order to release the information. We thought our mother would not agree to this because of her pride. The next day, we went back to the state hospital together, and I took Mary to the same office where I met Lydia. We encountered another woman, and I asked, "Where's Lydia?" The woman said, "Who's Lydia?" I explained, "I was here yesterday and met a woman who gave me this file number, and she told me her name was Lydia." The woman said, "That can't be. I worked here all day yesterday, I do all the records work, and there's no one that works here named Lydia." My sister and I believe Lydia must have been an angel who provided me with the file number.

Mary and I left the hospital. We had the file number we needed. We went together to tell our mother what we did. She got very angry and said, "Why do you want to go and open this up? It was nobody's business." I said, "Mom, grandpa came to me, and he wants to use this information to help his son Vince. It's not for you or me to decide; it's for Uncle Vince."

My mother remained angry, but she agreed to go and get the court order. My Aunt Luz, Vince's wife, went with her.

After they got the court order, we got all the papers about my grandfather. That's how we found out that my grandfather had what they called "an organic disease." Back then, they didn't know what was wrong with my grandfather or my uncle. They called it an organic disease, a brain disease, but it was early onset Alzheimer's.

My grandfather died from Alzheimer's, and my uncle was able to live longer, because the doctors then knew how to treat him. My Uncle Vince died at age fifty. Doctors knew that it was a hereditary disease. He died at St. Joseph's Medical Center in Stockton, California.

Prior to his death, the disease had progressed so much that Uncle Vince was placed for a while in the same state hospital where my grandfather had died. Uncle Vince's behavior regressed as he came closer to dying. With Alzheimer's, you can't eat by yourself anymore, you can't walk on your own, and you can't do anything. You may not even know your own family. Uncle Vince knew my Aunt Luz here and there. He died by himself, however, because that day when my aunt went downstairs to have lunch, there was a fire drill. The hospital doors locked, and she couldn't return to his room. During that time, Uncle Vince died. Although Aunt Luz wasn't with him when he died, she was able to take care of matters after that.

Later, Aunt Luz's son Macario got early onset Alzheimer's, and he died at age fifty. Then my mother's sister Rufina Hernandez Canales died at age fifty-five from Alzheimer's. Some time later, my Aunt Rufina's two sons died of the same disease, both at the age of fifty. It is clearly evident that Alzheimer's is a hereditary disease in my family.

Earlier in this story, I said that our God is the God of the living. These testimonies support what I mean when I say we never die. We have our life today and when we pass away from this life, we go on to the next life, but our spirit lives on forever. My grandfather came to me in spirit and moved me to get his medical documents, which ultimately led to our family finding out the true story behind his death. In addition, his medical documents helped assist doctors in determining a diagnosis for my Uncle Vincent.

I ask the reader, no matter what faith you are, please pray for our family. Currently, my Aunt Luz's grandson Max is undergoing tests. He needs our prayers. Please stop reading and say a prayer for him and our family.

John 14:12-14 says:

Amen, amen, I say to you, whoever believes in me will do the works that I do, and will do greater ones than these, because I am going to the Father. And whatever you ask in my name, I will do, so that the Father may be glorified in the Son. If you ask anything of me in my name, I will do it.

A Visit to Paradise

People say there is no Purgatory, but I believe there is. I believe there is a place that we go to after death where we have to be sorry for the littlest sin we have committed and just as sorry for the biggest sin we have committed. We must be purified before we enter into Heaven. Purgatory is a paradise where we can be cleansed.

One day while praying to the Lord, I asked to see Purgatory. And all at once, there it was. I was actually in Purgatory. It was a beautiful garden. I saw my grandmother there, and I could see others I knew who had died. They were all kneeling and praying.

When my grandmother died, she had no legs. They both had been amputated, due to diabetes. But in this garden, she had both legs and feet. She was kneeling and praying and was dressed in all white. Almost everyone was dressed in white, and everyone was whole. The smell of roses lingered in the atmosphere, and a bright light shone above everyone. The light reminded me that Jesus said, "I am the light of the world." A crystal clear mist also hovered over the garden, and I could see that all the people were praying. Some of them were singing as well. The music and the people singing and praying simultaneously sounded so beautiful. I thought, *Yes, this is where we come to be cleansed. Some of us have to be here longer than others, but it's not a bad place.*

I believe that Purgatory is another representation of the Communion of Saints. I believe that some of us have a time there, and that God uses us elsewhere according to His will and purpose. We don't always understand God's ways, and in this world, we never will. We will understand, however, when we die. I feel that Jesus called this place Paradise, but we call it Purgatory. It is a place we will go to where Jesus will be with us.

Remember, in the scriptures in Luke 23:42-43, the thief asked our Lord:

> ..."Jesus, remember me when you come into your kingdom." He replied to him, "Amen, I say to you, today you will be with me in Paradise."

Ball of Fire and the El Camino

Most of my married life with my husband Rudy was happy. We were married for twenty-six years and I can say that probably only the last ten years were miserable. I mean that. It was not a good situation, due to Rudy's alcohol addiction, but I was committed. I wanted to stick it out, but that didn't happen.

One day Rudy went out drinking and burned up the engine in his El Camino. I remember he took it in to be fixed, but the cost for repair was six hundred dollars.

After we saved and scraped up the money, Rudy went to get his car out of the shop and brought it home. However, he was drinking again and called his cousins and took them for a ride. This time, he cracked the block. He broke his car again, right after getting it out of the shop. I thought, *God, how will he pay for this?* I remember that I just cried. Rudy felt real bad. He said, "Sally, I cracked the block in the engine, and now it won't start." I said, "What are you going to do?" Rudy replied,

"I can't do anything; I burned it up." I said, "Well, go try to start it, Rudy." He emphatically repeated, "It won't start," and he had his cousin tow it home.

That night when Rudy went to bed, I stayed up praying at the kitchen table with my family Bible, which Rudy had bought for me. We always had that Bible open in our home. I remember sitting there in despair not knowing what to do or how to pray. Rudy's El Camino was in the garage, broken, and I was crying and couldn't sleep. I was sitting there with the Bible and asked Jesus, "Jesus, show me the Holy Spirit. I want to see the Holy Spirit." I was crying and placed my hands on the Bible, saying, "Please, I want to see the Holy Spirit."

Suddenly, my hands started to glow. I saw shiny, running water—like diamonds—bright, beautiful diamonds in the water. Then, unexpectedly, it flowed from my hands and formed into a ball of fire. This ball of fire flashed like lightning, hit the ceiling, and started to spin. Through it came a voice that said, "I am the Lord thy God," and I remember looking at the fire and saying, "If you're God, then you can fix the truck." Immediately, it started moving around. It moved from one corner to another. It had great power and speed. I said, "Please fix the car."

The ball of fire then went out the back door and into the garage. I followed it. It went right into the motor. It hit the motor and the side of the truck and then went inside again. It moved with great speed and after it went back into the truck, it went back into the house. I followed it back in, and the door closed. Then the ball of fire started to speak to me.

I remember that the Lord told me, through this ball of fire, that the neighbor who lived a few houses from my house needed prayer. He also asked me to go to the hospital, because there was a priest there who needed prayer. I said to God, "Lord, when are you going to heal Rudy? When is he going to change, Lord? When is he going to stop drinking? When is he, Lord?" The Lord answered me through the ball of fire. He said, "He will crawl to me on his belly, and I will save him." I will never forget that.

I couldn't wait for Rudy to wake up. I told him, "Rudy, the Lord came to me last night." I would share everything that the Lord was doing in my life with Rudy. It was hard for him, but he believed me, because he saw things happen just as God would declare. I said, "You know, Rudy, God fixed your truck. It's fixed." He said, "Sally, the motor is burned; why are you saying this?" I said, "Because God came in a ball of fire, and I saw the ball of fire go into the garage and hit the truck, and I know it is going to start. Go on out there and start the truck." Rudy said, "Okay, I'll go out there."

Rudy went out to the garage and got into the truck. The truck started—he couldn't believe it. He said, "I probably didn't do what I thought I did." I said, "No, Rudy, there was something wrong, just as you said. But I tell you, God came through a ball of fire to show me the power of the Holy Spirit and the power of prayer. Rudy can't you believe that?" Rudy believed it, but he didn't know how to share the news with his cousins when they all came over to help fix the car. I heard Rudy trying to tell them. He said, "Well, Sally prayed." But then he said,

"You know what? Maybe we didn't . . . maybe it was not. . . ." He went on, but he knew the truth. And you know, I will never forget those words when God said, "He will crawl to me on his belly, and I will heal him." See God is going to heal Rudy. He's going to be healed. And when God heals him, whenever that is, Rudy is going to find peace and love and joy and happiness. He's a good man and deserves to have some happiness in his life.

I now know that if God spoke to Moses through a burning bush, he could speak to me through a ball of fire. We read in Exodus 3:2-4:

> There an angel of the LORD appeared to him in fire flaming out of a bush. As he looked on, he was surprised to see that the bush, though on fire, was not consumed. So Moses decided, "I must go over to look at this remarkable sight, and see why the bush is not burned."

> When the LORD saw him coming over to look at it more closely, God called out to him from the bush, "Moses! Moses!" He answered, "Here I am."

From Dirty, Miry Water to Clear Blue Water

"Ask and it will be given to you; seek and you will find; knock and the door will be opened to you. For everyone who asks, receives; and the one who seeks, finds; and to the one who knocks, the door will be opened." (Matthew 7:7-8)

After I had moved to Florida, and my daughter Jeana had come home from her six-month deployment, we decided to buy a home together. Jeana had seen a new development going up on her way to work—the Navy, where she served for twenty years—and asked me if I wanted to see the new houses. I agreed, and we both went to check them out.

We looked at the three available models, which were well-built brick homes. After much prayer, we decided on the one we wanted to buy. Because we were going to buy the biggest lot, we had to make a down payment, so that the builder could put a sold tag on it. We signed papers, answered the questions, and so forth, to begin the credit check and employment verification process.

While waiting for the approval, one morning my daughter Jeana came into my bedroom and woke me up. She asked me to go with her to see the water at the home construction site. She said, "Mom, please come and see the water; it doesn't look good at all. It's dirty, it's very dirty." I said, "Well, we have thirty days, Jeana. We don't have to buy it. We can still get out of it." She said, "Just come and see. Bring your holy water,

mom." So I did. I took the holy water but I didn't know what
she was talking about until I got there. The water was quite
ugly. It looked like it even had oil in it. It was very dirty. Jeana
asked, "How are we going to have a home built with the water
so dirty? Our dining room will be facing the water and so will
the front room." She was very upset and I, too, thought, *You're*
right. We can't live in a home that has dirty and miry water. I
said to Jeana, "You know what? Let's just ask God. Let's ask
the Lord to change the miry water into clear blue water. He
can make it happen." I took the holy water and sprinkled it all
around, especially in the water. I also sprinkled the holy water
throughout the property. After doing that, I got on my knees
and asked the Lord to please hear our prayers. I prayed one
Our Father and one Hail Mary, and I asked God, "If you want
this home to be ours, please clear the water." I also told the
Lord that I knew He wanted the best for us and let Him know
how much we loved and trusted Him.

We went home, and I said to Jeana, "Now, we have to give
the situation to God. We must trust him and wait and see what
He does. We'll give it a few days or a week or so." I reminded
Jeana that we had thirty days.

About two weeks after we prayed and asked God to change
the miry water, I came home from work and before I went to
bed, Jeana met me at the door. She said, "Mom, come and see."
I said, "What, Jeana?" She said, "Before you go to bed, I want
you to come and see the water." She couldn't even tell me what
was going on. So we both got in the car to go check out what

was going on with the water. It was raining hard that day, but I went to see it. I couldn't believe my eyes. Hundreds of whirlpools were spinning around and around in the water, real fast. I remember the joy I felt knowing that God was doing a great miracle for us. I also remember that we both cried, knowing that it was God who blessed the water and changed it to blue water. It was our sign that we were supposed to buy the house. It was a wonderful place to live, and God again heard our prayers.

We closed in December 1989, and spent our first Christmas in our beautiful new home. Because the Lord turned the water from dirty, miry water into clear blue water, we knew that it was His will that we live there.

If Jesus could change water into wine, He absolutely could change dirty, muddy water into clear, clean, blue water for us. John 2:7-11 says:

> Jesus told them, "Fill the jars with water." So they filled them to the brim. Then he told them, "Draw some out now and take it to the headwaiter." So they took it. And when the headwaiter tasted the water that had become wine, without knowing where it came from (although the servers who had drawn the water knew), the headwaiter called the bridegroom and said to him, "Everyone serves good wine first, and then when people have drunk freely, an inferior one; but you have kept the good wine until now." Jesus did this as the beginning of his signs in Cana in Galilee and so revealed his glory, and his disciples began to believe in him.

Lightning Pierces Hands and Feet

In the winter of 1996, something happened to me with no explanation, even after asking the Lord why it happened. It was raining hard that day, and lots of lighting flashed through the sky. I remember sitting and working in my office when, suddenly, from the corner of my eyes I saw a bolt of lightning come through the ceiling and pierce my feet. Then, once more, another bolt of lightning shot down and struck my hands. I felt like the lightning bolts penetrated directly through the centers of both my feet and hands. I sat there, stunned, and prayed to the Lord. I wasn't afraid but didn't understand the reason why this incident occurred.

Into the next year, I remained concerned about this event but did not let it worry me and left it in God's hands.

Not a Heart Attack but a Message from God

On June 26, 1997, while at work and speaking with the owner of the business, my niece Sylvia, I felt a piercing, stabbing pain in my heart. The pain was so intense and sharp that it knocked me to the floor. Sylvia immediately called an ambulance. After the paramedics arrived and checked my blood pressure, which was very high, they said I needed to get to the hospital right away. I wasn't afraid this time either, because I felt a strong, calm presence with me.

The paramedic put an IV in my arm and called the hospital. I heard him say, ". . . possible heart attack." St. Joseph's Medical Center was only two blocks from the office. I felt as though God was preparing me for something, but I didn't understand what. I thought, *first my feet, then my hands, and now my heart.* I remember praying and saying to God, "If this can bring glory to You, then Your will be done."

Not until August did I understand why I went through these extraordinary experiences. The Blessed Mother explained it all to me while riding on the airplane during my trip to Medjugorje. She told me to write it all down, and I did. However, I cannot share the reason until the right time—God's time.

It's been thirteen years, and it's still not the right time to share. Until then, I will wait on the Lord for His direction as to how and when to share the details of these amazing, extraordinary experiences.

Feeling the Crucifixion Pain

I want to share that in 1997, a few months before my trip to Medjugorje, and on the feast of Corpus Christi, I woke up feeling sharp pains in my feet about three o'clock in the morning. At the time, I lived with my friend Vicki who I met through her two children Mia and Jose. They were in my youth group at church, and Vicki attended the prayer group I led. When I screamed, Vicki came into my bedroom to see what was the matter. I'll never forget this experience, for I had either a vision or a dream of the crucifixion.

When I woke up, my feet were positioned together as if I was being crucified. I felt sharp, boring pains in my feet, as if they were being pierced with large nails. The pain was intense.

I noticed my arms were outstretched from my sides, with my body imitating the form of a cross. I remember telling Vicki why I had screamed, and she thought it was best for me to stay home from work that day so that I could recuperate. I did as she suggested.

Again, why this extraordinary event happened, I don't know. I do believe, however, that it had something to do with my spiritual journey.

8
Lord, Teach Me About Marriage

After twenty-six years of marriage to Rudy, I finally decided to get a divorce in 1986. It was one of the most difficult decisions I had ever had to make in my life. One reason it was so difficult was that I had no confidence in my ability to take care of myself, and my son, who was sixteen at the time and still living at home. I knew that God would help me with my decision, but I had so many insecurities.

After much prayer that same year, I decided to move to Jacksonville, Florida, with my daughter Jeana to care for her seven-month-old daughter, Jacquelynn. Jeana had been serving in the Navy and, at that time, was ordered to go on a six-month tour. I thought that the move to Florida would be a good opportunity for me.

Six months of caring for my granddaughter went by fast. During that time, I would stop at the church and pray for the children and grandchildren I had left behind in California. My son had decided to stay behind and live with my oldest daughter, Cynthia, as he had only one more year before he graduated high school. It was nice living in Florida, and I met many wonderful people there. I prayed a lot while Jeana was away, seeking God's will for what I would do when she'd return home.

When Jeana came home later that year, I decided I'd better find a job. I was fast on a 10-key, so PIE, a trucking company, hired me to key in the truckloads as they came in every night. I was handed a list of truck numbers from all over the states, and I keyed the numbers into the computer, tracking how many loads came in a day and from which states. I worked nights, so I was able to go to Mass every morning after work. I had a picture I carried of Rudy and me when we were married. It was taken when we were happy. I say that, because we both looked happy in the picture. After Mass, I would take the picture out of my purse and go to the Blessed Sacrament and pray the Rosary for my children and their father. Never would I have thought in a thousand years we'd get a divorce; I didn't believe in divorce, but it happened.

One day during my daily Mass at Sacred Heart Catholic Church, I was kneeling in front of the Blessed Sacrament praying my Rosary and had a vision. I had been asking the Lord what to do, if I should get an annulment or not. In this vision, I saw Rudy and me when we got married in the church. We were kneeling before the altar, and the priest was there, representing God. Rudy and I were bound together in what seemed to be a cocoon. We were as one. As the vision progressed, I saw that Rudy started to untangle himself from the cocoon. I could see him then floating through the sky away from me. He was leaving the cocoon where I was, and was drifting miles away. I realized then that he was in Stockton, California, and I was in Jacksonville, Florida. Although Rudy was a great distance away from me and the cocoon, I could see us bound together by what appeared to be angel hair. The angel hair was wrapped around Rudy's waist and my waist, binding us together.

God revealed to me that the angel hair symbolized the bond of marriage that held Rudy and me together. The Sacrament of Marriage is very powerful. Because it is such a strong sacrament, a couple can overcome any battle or sickness that may come their way, if only they allow the graces to flow and the Lord to intervene in their marriage.

God also showed me how strong the marriage bond is by showing me weights. First, He placed a thousand pounds on the bond, then two thousand, then three thousand and, finally, ten thousand pounds. Nothing could break this bond of matrimony, no matter how heavy. The angel hair manifested once more, and God told me that I had a choice. He showed me a very large pair of scissors with the word "Annulment" inscribed on them. The scissors were opened, and God showed me that cutting through the bond of angel hair was the only way to break the marriage sacrament.

It was my choice to continue praying and reel Rudy back in or get an annulment that would set me free. God has shown me throughout the years that the angel hair I saw was very thin but very strong. He showed me that if I decided to pray Rudy back into my life, that Rudy would have to pray with me because of the marriage sacrament and the two of us being one in the Lord. Through prayer, the angel hair bond could thicken, and nothing would be able to break it. I prayed for many years before the divorce and eventually felt that it was time to be set free. I made the decision to get an annulment, which was granted to me on April 2, 2003.

The Sacrament of Marriage represents a domestic church of God. Jesus told us to look at two people in love to see the love He has for His church. People have asked me why I got married in the church on March 19, 1982, and I will never forget the reason I did. First, I'd like to explain to you that Rudy and I were married for twenty-two years before we got married in the Catholic Church. I know today that getting married again in the Church wasn't what God wanted for us. I always jumped ahead whenever God asked me to do something, believing I knew when anything was from Him. As a result, I would proceed without praying and asking Him for guidance.

For example, once during prayer, God spoke to me and said, "You will lead my people out of the desert." I thought He wanted me to bring my sister Louise back to live in Stockton. Louise lived in the desert in Lancaster, so I went to visit her and asked her to move back to Stockton, but that was not what God meant. Louise had a beautiful home and didn't want to move. I was hurt, but then God gave me an understanding of what He meant. He meant that there are many people in the world who have lost their faith, and He was going to use me to lead them back into that faith. I know that now. Coincidently, when God said through a priest who was praying over me at a prayer meeting, "Mary! Mary! God wants to change your name to Martha, and in your second marriage you and your husband will lead many to God, to Christ," I took that literally and believed that God was talking about Rudy and me getting married in the Catholic Church. We were already married but not through the Church. I thought that would be my second marriage, but it wasn't. You see, that's how I was. Whenever God would tell me something, I wanted to obey him. I have since learned, through the many mistakes I have made in my lifetime, to simply wait on the Lord. Psalms 46:11 says,

> ..."Be still and confess that I am God!
> I am exalted among the nations,
> exalted on the earth."

I am now too old to get married again and I'm happy being alone. But if there is someone who God would bring into my life, then He will let me know. The man would have to be a man of God who loves the Lord more than he loves me.

I had to share this vision about marriage in this book. Isn't it beautiful? Can you envision what God showed me? I would love to get an artist to put it on paper. It was a beautiful revelation of marriage. Maybe some day I will find someone to draw it for me. Once God shows me something in my mind and it touches my heart and becomes reality, I know it is the truth. Marriage is the mirror of Christ's love for His bride—the Church.

> For this reason a man shall leave his father and mother [and be joined to his wife], and the two shall become one flesh. So they are no longer two but one flesh. Therefore what God has joined together, no human being must separate. (Mark 10:7-8)

9
One Day You Will Wash My Feet

"How beautiful upon the mountains
are the feet of him who brings glad tidings,
Announcing peace, bearing good news,
announcing salvation, and saying to Zion,
"Your God is King!"
(Isaiah 52:7)

Once at a Cursillo, I was thinking about the feet of Christ. The Cursillo was in Copperopolis, near Stockton, California. By custom there, the head cooks would help wash the candidates' feet. I was head of the kitchen at that Cursillo. One of the rules that I had instituted was that we would pray the Rosary each of the four days we were there, every hour on the hour. No matter what we were doing, we would pray a decade of the Rosary together. Whether we were outside or in the chapel, we would wait until we came back into the kitchen to pray another decade. When we were serving breakfast or lunch, and after dinner as soon as everybody would leave, we would pray a decade of the Rosary again together. We said many Rosaries during that weekend. Saturday night was the night that we washed the candidates' feet.

Years ago, in a related story, when my oldest daughter, Cynthia, was sixteen years old, she and my family would attend Mass together. It was Holy Thursday, the day our priest would choose certain people in the parish to have their feet washed. He would pick twelve from the congregation. The priest would call them ahead of time, so that they could be prepared to go up for the ceremony. All the participants sat in the front rows. Before Mass that day, I remember Cindy and I had a disagreement. I was so hurt and I scolded her, which then made her cry and made us all late for Mass. We always sat in one of the front rows at Mass, but this time, because we were late, we had to sit in the back. As I was sitting in the back, I was watching the people who Father had picked to have their feet washed. He called out their names, and they walked to the front of the church with their socks off, ready to have their feet washed.

I remember I started to cry. I said, "You know, Lord, I've been working for you for a long time. I should have been one of those chosen to have my feet washed. Why didn't Father ask me to get my feet washed?"

I was hurt. I remember just sobbing about this and having a moment of what I now realize was self-pity. I thought, *God, I should be up there.* I truly wanted my feet washed. I felt that I needed my feet washed, as I had been going through so much that year. I was constantly on my knees, praying. I was so brokenhearted, and then I heard a voice. I can't stress to you enough that in the Bible, God says, "My sheep know my voice." And I know His voice. The Lord said to me, while I was crying, "One day, you will wash my feet." And I responded in a soft voice, "Lord, how am I going to wash your feet?" He said, "One day, you will wash my feet."

And now getting back to the Cursillo. That Saturday about seven o'clock, the cooking staff and I were praying the Rosary, and I was looking out towards the Royal Room, which was the place where they did all the presentations during the Cursillo. This Cursillo took place during the fall, when colorful autumn leaves covered the ground and sidewalks. I remember that I saw a man walking toward the chapel wearing a white robe, you know, like the kind that Jesus and the priests wear. He was walking, and I could see his feet. He was barefoot. He had leaves flying up around his feet as he walked along the path. I wanted to say, "Look, there's Jesus!" but I didn't say anything. That night, I heated the water because it was cool outside, and I wanted it to be nice and warm for the participants' feet. We started to wash the candidates' feet, and when we got to one particular girl, named Anna, I will never forget what happened. Anna had a beautiful voice, and her husband Beto played the guitar. Together they sang for the church. Anna was a wonderful person. That night, when I knelt down to wash her feet, her feet weren't hers—they were Jesus' feet. They were men's feet, and they had leaves on them, just like I saw on the man in the white robe walking along the path earlier that day. As the memory of him came back to me, I heard the voice of the Lord in my heart and in my ear. He asked, "Remember when I told you that one day you will wash my feet?" Well, this was the day when I washed the feet of Jesus, as He said I would. Jesus allowed me to wash His feet. I remember I shared this testimony with Anna later. She said, "When you put the water on my feet, Sally, I felt Jesus was present and ever so close to me."

How about that? God blessed me with yet one more grace of our Lord, Jesus Christ—the everlasting Grace that continues to flow among us.

> If I, therefore, the master and teacher, have washed your feet, you ought to wash one another's feet. I have given you a model to follow, so that as I have done for you, you should also do. (John 13:14)

10

The Power of Praying the Rosary

P raying the Rosary, to me, is very powerful. After Mass each morning, I pray my Rosary on the way to work. Sometimes if I don't have time to pray in the morning, I'll pray a decade in intervals throughout the day. I believe that praying the Rosary is repeating scripture, because the words of the Rosary came from scripture. In Luke 1:26-28, it reads:

In the sixth month, the angel Gabriel was sent from God to a town of Galilee called Nazareth, to a virgin betrothed to a man named Joseph, of the house of David, and the virgin's name was Mary. And coming to her, he said, "Hail, favored one! The Lord is with you."

Also, in Luke 1:41, it reads:

When Elizabeth heard Mary's greeting, the infant leaped in her womb, and Elizabeth, filled with the holy Spirit, cried out in a loud voice and said, "Most blessed are you among women, and blessed is the fruit of your womb."

"The Blessed Mother"
Illustrated by Pat Wilke Tadena

These are the words we use when we pray the Rosary. For me, the Rosary is like a weapon used as armor against Hell. I know that many of you readers aren't Catholic, but I would like to share with you "The Canticle of Mary." Luke 1:45-55 says:

"Blessed are you who believed that what was
spoken to you by the Lord would be fulfilled."
And Mary said:
"My soul proclaims the greatness of the Lord;
my spirit rejoices in God my savior.
For he has looked upon his handmaid's lowliness;
behold, from now on will all ages call me blessed.
The Mighty One has done great things for me,
and holy is his name.
His mercy is from age to age
to those who fear him.
He has shown might with his arm,
dispersed the arrogant of mind and heart.
He has thrown down the rulers from their thrones
but lifted up the lowly.
The hungry he has filled with good things;
the rich he has sent away empty.
He has helped Israel his servant,
remembering his mercy,
according to his promise to our fathers,
to Abraham and to his descendants forever."
(emphasis added)

During a certain period of my life, every time I'd get a call about praying for someone who was sick, I would go to my room, kneel down, and pray a Rosary for a special healing for that person. I often prayed four or five Rosaries a day.

Praying the Rosary throughout the years has brought many graces to me and has given me so much peace. Whenever I need an answer, I pray the Rosary, and I most always receive an answer.

Praying the Rosary

Rosaries Turn Gold

There was a time when I lived in Florida when all my friends were taking trips to Medjugorje, but I couldn't. Everyone would come back and share stories of their experiences, such as how their rosaries turned gold when the Blessed Mother appeared in the church or in the fields. I wanted so badly to go but couldn't afford the time or money. As an alternative, I made the decision to send my rosary with a friend. I asked her to see if it would turn gold for me. I thought that would be wonderful if the Blessed Mother would turn my rosary gold just as she had for so many others.

When my friend returned after her trip, she called me and told me that she had my rosary and, yes, it had turned gold. Anxiously, I set up a time and place to meet with her, so she could give me my rosary. Little did I know at that time, however, that the rosary I had sent to Medjugorje wasn't for me but for someone else.

I met with my friend and she showed me the rosary, it was so beautiful. It was really very gold in color. I remember feeling so proud that I owned a rosary that had been blessed by our Blessed Mother. My daughter Jeana and I had plans to stop at Taco Bell to eat after I picked up my rosary, so I put it in my jacket pocket.

While at Taco Bell, Jeana noticed that the rosary was partially hanging out of my pocket. Right away, I made sure it was completely inside my pocket. When I got up to leave after we ate, I felt as though someone had reached into my pocket and pulled out the rosary. I patted my pocket, and felt it there, so I got into my car, drove off, and went home.

As soon as I got home, I reached into my pocket for the rosary and, to my dismay, it wasn't there. I immediately drove back to Taco Bell and frantically searched the restaurant and even looked in the parking lot. I found nothing. I then said a prayer, "Lord, where is my rosary?" I waited on the Lord and only felt peace in my heart after realizing that the rosary must have been meant for someone else who needed it more than I. I believe God sent an angel to get the rosary and take it to the one who needed it more.

Eventually, God provided me with opportunities to go to Medjugorje. I have had the grace to go five times and was blessed in many ways. During some of those trips to Medjugorje, I received other rosaries that had turned gold, but none of them were meant for me.

In 1997, I was the youth minister for St. Gertrude's church. I had fifty young people in my youth group, and I was able to take fifteen youth and ten adults on a trip to Medjugorje. They experienced many graces. God's grace is everlasting.

The adults paid their own way for the trip, and the youth who weren't able to go worked many fundraisers to help the fifteen who were able to go. We worked those fundraisers for two years to make enough money for the fifteen youth. That, in itself, was a big effort for those young people, and I was so proud of all of them. They worked as if they all were going on the trip.

This reminds me that once while praying in front of the Blessed Sacrament, a prayer came to my mind and heart: "Lord, could I have enough kids join the youth group, so with hard work we will be able to attend the next World Youth Day in France?" I went on to say, "Lord, I only have ten young people who have joined, but I will need more if we are going to get there." I then heard a voice come from the tabernacle. It said, "I only had twelve." Something inside of me knew then that I would have enough youth. Every week thereafter, more new youth came and joined the group until there were fifty. Hallelujah! We went to World Youth Day in France—to Medjugorje—that year, 1997.

I remember that, yes, it was a hard task the Lord had asked of me to take this large group to Medjugorje; but it was very rewarding. One of the young men in my youth group, Lewis Huanta, experienced a change in his life. He felt the Lord's presence like never before and wanted to do so much more for the youth group. His life surely changed for the better. Although it was hard for him to express his feelings to his peers, he did share everything with our Pastor, Father Charles Countie.

During our trip, one of the girls had left her purse in a taxicab. Her wallet had more than three hundred dollars in it. She was upset because she didn't know who it was that should be called. We told her that once the taxicab driver saw her purse, that he would bring it back. She just cried. I know that she didn't believe the driver would come back, but hours later, a taxi pulled up. The cab driver came out and had the purse in his hand. He said, "You," pointing at the young girl, "left your purse in my car. I couldn't bring it back any sooner than now. I hope that you weren't too worried." We offered him some money for bringing the purse back. At first he said, "No, thank you." However, after we told him he could use it for gas, with some hesitation he took, I think, twenty dollars. The money was still in the girl's purse in the same place she kept it, and it looked like the gentleman didn't even go through the purse. The people in Medjugorje are very kind and honest.

Father Charles also went with us on the trip. When he came back, one of the parishioners, Louis Hernandez, heard that Father wished he had bells for his church like those seen in Medjugorje. Louis then gifted bells to the church in memory of his wife Christina Hernandez.

There were many tears from the youth after this trip, as they had each experienced something special. Many went to confession for the first time in a long time. While in Medjugorje, some experienced the Sun spinning and changing colors. Others saw the stars fall from the sky when they announced that the Blessed Mother was there. We had the honor of staying in Mirjana, home to one of the visionaries, and the honor of seeing Pope John Paul II, who is now closer to sainthood. It was a blessed year.

From this same visit in 1997, I had a very beautiful and special rosary that had turned gold. After returning from Medjugorje, I was kneeling down and praying one Wednesday at a prayer meeting. A family came in to ask for prayer for their daughter who had just found out that day that she had cervical cancer. They came to pray and to ask the Lord to please heal her. As I knelt, I could hear a voice say to me, "Give her the rosary; it's not for you, it's for her." I said, "Why do I always have to give my rosaries away? I want this one to be mine. I have another rosary that isn't gold but has been blessed by our Blessed Mother." The voice then said, "Give the rosary to her. She is going to be healed." I got up and told everyone who was there that night what happened. I told them I heard a voice, and I believed it was the Blessed Mother speaking to my heart and telling me to give the rosary to the young lady and that she would be healed.

The young lady took the rosary. We all prayed over her and asked God to heal the cancer in her cervix. We didn't see the young lady again for a while. After some time, she came in one day to thank us for our prayers. She was healed, and her parents remained parishioners at St. Gertrude's church. The young lady still has the rosary. She was completely healed, and the cancer never came back. Mark 5:22-23 says:

> One of the synagogue officials, named Jairus, came forward. Seeing him he fell at his feet and pleaded earnestly with him, saying, "My daughter is at the point of death. Please, come lay your hands on her that she may get well and live."

My Brother and the Rosary

During a period of twenty-five years when my brother, Louis, was away from the Catholic Church, lots of things happened to him and his family. I thought, *What must I do, Lord, to bring my brother back to the Catholic faith, so that we can pray again as a family?* Then I started praying the Rosary for Louis to come back to the Catholic Church. He was involved with other churches during that time. In fact, he was so in love with the Lord that he went from church to church. He learned the Bible scriptures, the Old and New Testaments, and he earnestly wanted to be a preacher.

When I started praying the Rosary for his return to the church, I called him to let him know what I was doing. He just laughed but also told me he'd never come back to the Catholic Church. He said, "Sally I don't want to hurt you, but I'm not coming back." He went on to say that he was happy in the church he was in. If I remember right, he was in a Four Corners Church in San Jose. I somehow knew in my heart that he would be back, so I continued to pray.

I believe so much in the power of the Rosary when I am repeating the scripture over and over, "Hail Mary full of grace, the Lord is with you. Blessed are you among women and blessed is the fruit of your womb, Jesus," that I started praying for Louis. One night while praying for him, I had a vision. I saw Louis dressed in a white alb and preaching at St. Gertrude's Catholic Church—the church where we all were baptized and made our Confirmation and all of the Sacraments. I saw my mother and sisters in the front row listening to him. The next day, I called Louis and told him about the vision, and he didn't say anything other than, "Sally, I don't have any plans to come back to the Catholic Church."

Time passed, and I continued to pray for my brother. Then, in 1993, I got a surprising phone call. It was my sister-in-law Helen, and she said, "Sally, your brother wants you to know that he is going to need your help in becoming a deacon in the Catholic Church." I said, "What? What am I supposed to do?" She explained that they needed me to ask Father Charles Countie, the pastor at St. Gertrude's, if he would sponsor Louis. They were planning to come back to the Church but didn't know Father as well as I did. She said, "Sally, we really need your help." At first I thought, *Am I hearing correctly? My brother wants to be a deacon?* I didn't know what to think. Helen told me she'd call me back to find out what Father said. I sat there thinking, *Blessed Mother you knew my brother would come back.* I was so happy. Then the phone rang, and again it was my sister-in-law. She said, "Sally, do you remember the vision you had a long time ago?" And I said, "Helen, I was just thinking about that vision." "Well, I believe what you saw years ago is happening," her voice cracked as she replied. We both started to cry, and then I said, "Helen, God's will is being done."

The next day, I went to speak to Father Charles and I asked him if he would sponsor Louis to become a deacon. He responded, "Sally, because he's your brother, yes, I will sponsor him." He then made an appointment with my brother. Louis attended the classes, and on September 13, 2003, he was ordained a deacon. This was a great day for our entire family. My mother, and my sisters and I were there, just as I saw in the vision. God is good.

My brother preaches once a month at St. Gertrude's Catholic Church, and he is now the Catholic Chaplain for the California Youth Authority. Today he preaches to about fifty young men every Sunday and helps them during the week. I'm very proud of my brother. God allowed me to see this vision in 1970, thirty-three years before Louis became a deacon, so that I could continue to pray with faith. There was no doubt. I simply believed. 1 Thessalonians 5:15-18 reads:

> See that no one returns evil for evil; rather, always seek what is good [both] for each other and for all. Rejoice always. Pray without ceasing. In all circumstances give thanks, for this is the will of God for you in Christ Jesus.

Desperately Needed a Job

Standing by the cross of Jesus were his mother and his mother's sister, Mary the wife of Clopas, and Mary of Magdala. When Jesus saw his mother and the disciple there whom he loved, he said to his mother, "Woman, behold, your son." Then he said to the disciple, "Behold, your mother." And from that hour the disciple took her into his home. (John 19:25-27)

In 1979, three of my daughters were attending St. Mary's High School, and I was faced with having to pay all of their tuition before my oldest, Cynthia, could graduate. I badly needed a job so that I could help pay the school. I had worked at the Cannery during July and August, but it wasn't until April when I received a letter from the school stating that all tuition had to be paid before report cards would be sent out. It also stated that tuition for all graduates had to be paid in full before graduation. That meant that I had to come up with money I didn't have. In addition, two of my children were attending St. Gertrude's Elementary School. I thought, *Where can I find a job, so I can help Rudy with the tuition for both schools?*

Graduation was only two months away, so I got down on my knees and prayed the Rosary. While I was praying, I asked the Blessed Mother to intercede with me to the Father for help with finding a job. I remember thinking, *Where do I find a job? I have to work. I have to earn money to pay the balance of the tuition so my kids can stay in Catholic school.* I prayed and asked the Blessed Mother, "Please, show me where to go." I waited quietly, while on my knees at the side of my bed with my head down, to hear something from the Lord. Instead, I had a vision, and this is what I saw.

I saw myself pushing a cart down a hallway. The cart looked like the kind you see at the laundromats—big carts that you can fold your clothes in and haul them out to your car. *What does this mean?* I thought. In the vision, I also saw a chapel with a Tabernacle in it where the Blessed Sacrament is kept. I wasn't sure what the Blessed Mother was trying to show me.

The very next day I received a phone call from a woman named Lucia. At that time, Lucia was a friend from church who years later became my daughter Shelby's mother-in-law. She said, "Sally, I heard you're looking for a job?" She went on to say, "Why don't you go to the La Sallette; they are hiring. I'm working there in the kitchen." I asked her, "Where is it and what is it?" She replied, "It's a convalescent home, a rehabilitation facility. It's very nice." She gave me the address, and I went over to put in an application for a job.

As I was about to leave the La Sallette after completing my application, a lady stepped out of the office and called, "Sally, wait, we're going to hire you. When can you start?" I curiously but graciously asked, "What am I going to do? Am I going to work in the kitchen?" She said, "No, you aren't going to work in the kitchen; we have enough help there. You are going to be responsible for the patients' rooms making sure the beds are tidy, and you are going to dust off the night stands and make sure they have clean towels in the bathrooms, and that everything is in place in their rooms." The patients' rooms were beautiful. Some of them had private rooms with their own bathrooms. My job was going to be to make sure everything was clean. I only had to change the pillowcases, not the sheets, and had to make sure the beds were made nicely. Someone else was responsible for changing the sheets on the beds. I said to the manager, "Okay, I can start tomorrow."

The manager wanted to give me a quick tour before I left. She showed me where they kept the supplies, and she brought out the cart they used for toting all the supplies. The cart held clean linens and towels on one side, and on the other dust cloths to wipe the night stands and Windex to clean the mirrors. What astonished me, though, was that it resembled the same cart I saw in my vision while praying the Rosary! My heart jumped with joy. Down the hall next to the linen closet was a Chapel with a Tabernacle, an altar, and a few pews. Again—everything was just as I saw in the vision.

Most of the patients at the home were Catholic. The lady who owned the business had a son who was a Catholic priest. He would come and celebrate Mass on special days, such as St. Patrick's Day, St. Joseph's Day, and Ascension Thursday. It was a very nice place, and the patients there seemed very happy.

I worked at La Sallette for one year and a half. After I quit, I often went to visit patients I had made friends with throughout my time there. Yes, this answer to prayer for a job was God's everlasting grace at work once more in my life—and I was able to pay the tuition for both schools. Proverbs 3:5-6 says,

> Trust in the LORD with all your heart,
> on your own intelligence rely not;
> In all your ways be mindful of him,
> and he will make straight your paths.

Innocent Babies Received in Heaven

Throughout my life, I've always made friends easily at work and during lunch breaks. Many years ago, during a summer job where I picked cherries with a friend, I became friends with another young woman named Joyce. The two of us got along well because we were around the same age.

While eating lunch one day, Joyce asked me what faith I was, and I told her I was a Catholic. She told me she was Catholic, too, but didn't go to church anymore. I then asked her why she stopped going to Mass. She explained that she stopped going since her baby girl had died. Everyone at the lunch table stopped to listen to her. She went on to tell us that her daughter, only four months old, had died of crib death. She said that she had taken her baby to St. Gertrude's Catholic Church to ask the pastor, Father Armand Mayville, if he would baptize her. She went on to say that Father Armand had told her to "take the carcass home." She just couldn't believe that father had called her baby girl a carcass. Joyce said that she left there brokenhearted, with her lifeless baby in her arms, never to return. I didn't know what to say, so I asked her if I could pray with her.

I could feel Joyce's sadness and couldn't find any words to comfort her. I only knew that I wanted to help her with her heartache. I told her that she had to forgive Father Armand, and that he hadn't meant to hurt her. I emphasized , "You took your baby who had died to church and wanted it baptized?" And she said, "Well, why couldn't he do it?" I said, "Well, for Catholics, the Sacrament of Baptism is the first step in a lifelong journey of commitment and discipleship. Whether we are baptized as infants or adults, it's the Church's way for us to come and be initiated into the Catholic Church and be embraced by the whole community of believers and God.

Joyce started to cry, then she asked, "Where is my baby? The Bible says that unless you're born again, you won't go to heaven." I thought that she was thinking about the scripture reading in John 3:5, "Jesus answered, 'Amen, amen, I say to you, no one can enter the kingdom of God without being born of water and Spirit.'" I then said to Joyce, "I'm going to go home tonight and I am going to ask the Lord where your baby is." She asked, "Do you think He will tell you?" I answered, "Well, I'm going to pray my Rosary, and I believe God will tell me. I know He will."

That night I prayed the penitential Rosary. This is a special Rosary that is said with one's arms outstretched while praying the Hail Mary prayers. I prayed with my whole heart, "Lord, you've got to let me know where Joyce's baby is, so I can go to work tomorrow and let her know." I was kneeling in my bedroom and, at about the third mystery of the Rosary, I heard the voice of the Lord say, "I am the living water, water, water." I kept praying, and I heard His voice once more. This time He said, "I've formed you in your mother's womb, in your mother's womb."

As I continued to pray, I heard the voice repeat, "I am the living water, water, water. I've formed you in your mother's womb, womb, womb." Immediately, I had a vision. I saw a baby in the mother's womb in the bag of waters, and the water was sparkling like diamonds, similar to the water I saw in my hands when I asked God to show me the Holy Spirit. My own interpretation of this vision tells me that the Lord was saying He was there with the baby in the Mother's womb. He was forming the baby, and there in the mother's womb the baby was submerged in the living waters. God was telling me that in the womb is where He was, just as the scriptures say, "I've formed you in your mother's womb."

God has already taken care of the baby's new life. Again, this is my own interpretation. I believe that God's mercy and grace is with the innocent, the unborn, and with all the babies who have died before they were baptized. I also believe that God was showing me that we are all predestined, and that He waits for those who can to come to Him willingly.

I went to work the next day and told Joyce about my vision. I also told her that her baby was in heaven with God, all the saints, and the angels.

This story is a testimony of God's everlasting grace once more in action. I never saw Joyce again, as I worked the cherry-picking job only that one particular summer. I don't know if Joyce ever went back to church or forgave Father Armand, but I do know that God knows.

Romans 8:28-30 reads:

> We know that all things work for good for those who love God, who are called according to his purpose. For those he foreknew he also predestined to be conformed to the image of his Son, so that he might be the first-born among many brothers. And those he predestined he also called; and those he called he also justified; and those he justified he also glorified.

Isaiah 49:15 says:

> Can a mother forget her infant,
> be without tenderness for the child of her womb?
> Even should she forget,
> I will never forget you.

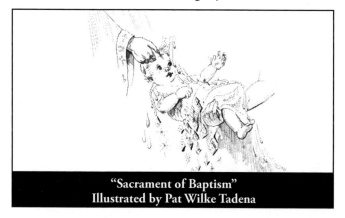

"Sacrament of Baptism"
Illustrated by Pat Wilke Tadena

Shelby's Healing

In the year 1977, my daughter Shelby was nine years old. One day while playing in the back yard, she fell out of a tree. She cried and told us her head hurt. We cared for her by putting ice on her head, and she seemed to be okay. Two weeks later, however, while she was sleeping one night, she had a seizure. I heard her father scream from her bedroom, "Sally, it's Shelby, something's wrong." We didn't know at the time what had caused the seizure.

Shortly thereafter, we took Shelby to the hospital and after many tests, the doctors diagnosed her with epilepsy. I couldn't believe it. The doctors decided to put her on two medications; 600 mg of Dilantin, and 600 mg of phenobarbital. Even with the medications, Shelby was still having the seizures. She would have at least two a day. She was in the second grade at St. Gertrude's Elementary School. She was a good reader and did well in math. Shelby was very smart.

One day the phone rang. It was the school secretary asking me to come into the office, because they needed to speak to me. Shelby's teacher and the school principal met with me, and they made the suggestion that I take Shelby out of school because she would fall asleep during class, due to the medicine she was taking. They also said that if Shelby were to have another seizure, it would scare her classmates. I understood and took her out of school.

We made an appointment with Dr. Dixon at the County Hospital so we could ask questions about the medication, thinking it was too strong for Shelby. She was so small and didn't weigh much. Again, she was only nine years old. Dr. Dixon recommended that we send Shelby to the UC in San Francisco, but told us she had to be screened through the County Hospital first. Shelby went through the series of tests at the County Hospital. The doctors ordered many x-rays, as well as an EEG of Shelby's head. Finally, they told us they discovered two blood clots in her brain. They also said she'd be able to have surgery to remove the blood clots, and that the seizures would stop. We had one more appointment to schedule and had a few days to wait.

While waiting for our last appointment with a team of doctors from San Francisco to see if they would accept Shelby's case, my sister Mary called me and asked if I could take the statue of Our Lady of Fatima to my house, because she was going away for a while. Mary had signed up in her parish to keep the statue of the Lady of Fatima at her house, but a while later, she was offered the opportunity to go to Mexico to visit the shrine of Our Lady of Guadalupe. Of course I agreed to take the statue for her. Parishioners soon brought the statue to my house, but I didn't know what my responsibility would actually be while it was in my house. It was going to be there for one week. I was told that I could invite the neighbors to come and pray for their families. I also thought I could use the time to pray for my daughter Shelby, so I asked the Blessed Mother if she'd bless all my family and intercede for Shelby and bring a healing to her, so she wouldn't suffer anymore with epilepsy.

The first day I had the statue, I bought a dozen red roses, put them in a vase with water, and placed the vase on the TV alongside the statue. I put all my children's pictures next to the statue and went down the street and invited some of my neighbors and friends to come and pray. Together we prayed our first Rosary. The next day, I noticed that all the roses were dried out. I was disappointed, as I had just bought them, but I threw them away and bought another dozen. That time they lasted. Someone who had read many books about the Blessed Virgin once told me the Blessed Mother loves the scent of roses and draws the scent out of them. I believe this, because I believe that the Blessed Virgin was really there in my home with the angels.

On the third night my family prayed the Rosary together, we prayed for Shelby to be healed. After everyone went to bed, I prayed another Rosary and asked the Blessed Mother to please intercede for Shelby, because if she had to have the surgery, it would be dangerous. That night, after praying, I went to bed and was awakened by music. I looked up and saw the statue floating down the hallway. Then I heard the Blessed Mother say to me, "Go back to sleep. You asked me to bless your family and that is what I'm doing." I fell back to sleep, and in the morning I got up and went to the front room to look at the statue. I noticed that there was wax on Shelby's picture, and there was one rose covered with wax lying across her picture. I remember kneeling down and thanking the Blessed Mother for what I witnessed during the night. I told her that I knew she came for Shelby and I just couldn't thank her enough. Once Shelby woke up, she came to me and said, "Mom, Jesus came to me last night. He came out of the cross in my room, and he said that I will never be sick again—no more seizures." There was a crucifix in Shelby's room with the station of the cross on it. I thought, *Jesus came to her?* She said, "I won't need to take anymore medicine. Jesus healed me."

When it was the day of our appointment with the team of doctors from the UC in San Francisco, Shelby said to me, "Mom, I don't have to take the medicine anymore, because Jesus healed me." I responded, "Well, let's wait until the doctors say so, okay? We'll tell them what happened, but Shelby, they might not believe us. Let's see what they say." Dr. Dixon, the head doctor at the County Hospital, called us in, and we sat there with the team of doctors. They told me again what they had found; that Shelby had two blood clots, and that they had accepted her case. Then I got up and said, "Doctors, my daughter Shelby has been healed." Then Shelby, at nine, got up and said, "Jesus came from the cross, and He said that I will never be sick again or have another seizure." I remember the head doctor from San Francisco said, "I can't digest what I just heard." Then he looked at me and said, "Your daughter is very sick and needs this surgery." He asked, "Is it your decision that your daughter Shelby Ann Quinones not have this surgery?" I replied, "Yes, doctor." He said this as if someone was recording what we were saying. Then we started to walk out, and Doctor

Dixon followed me out of the room. She said, "Mrs. Quinones, I too believe in miracles, but you must wean Shelby off of her medication. Every two weeks give her less. If you take her off all at once, she will get very sick, and it might make the seizures even stronger." I assured her I would. Then she took my hand and said, "Good Luck."

Shelby and I got home and I soon found her in the bathroom flushing her medication down the toilet. She looked at me and said once more, "Mom, Jesus said I will never have another seizure." She was right. Jesus did heal her. She never had another seizure. She was completely healed.

Shelby went back to school, got good grades, and remained in good health. God's everlasting grace was at work. I still have the rose with the wax on it. It is thirty-three years old. I keep it in a special box. I'll always treasure it, because I know that the Blessed Mother left it for me. She wanted me to know that, yes, she was there and, yes, she prayed for healing for my daughter Shelby, and she was healed completely.

I shared this story with the team who was in charge of taking the blessed statue around to family homes, and they asked me if they could share my story and wanted to show the picture. I told them yes, and that the following week we would go back to the doctor and share with them what happened as well. I did call to let them know what went on with the doctors, and they just praised the Lord.

I never could find the picture again and don't know if they remembered to give it back to me or not. I do remember, though, that I had all the pictures of my children next to the statue, and only Shelby's had wax on it. This again was God's everlasting grace at work.

Matthew 19:13-14 tells us:

> Then children were brought to him that he might lay his hands on them and pray. The disciples rebuked them, but Jesus said, "Let the children come to me, and do not prevent them; for the kingdom of heaven belongs to such as these."

Holy Redeemer Story

A final Rosary story is what I call my Holy Redeemer Story. Once, my friend Sister Maureen, a nun, and I went to San Jose to a healing Mass and a teaching. It was an all-day retreat. We left early in the morning for the retreat, but on our way back home later that evening, the weather turned bad. It was so foggy, we couldn't see left or right as we made our way down the highway. I couldn't stop because I didn't know if any cars were following behind me.

Sister Maureen got scared, and I was too. I could feel fear. I didn't know what was in front of me; I couldn't see the white line on the median or in which lane I was driving. The fog was very dense. I asked Sister if she could see anything on her side, and she said, "No, nothing." I said, "We need to pray. We need to start praying the Rosary right now. We need help."

Sister started praying the Rosary, and I started to pray with her. I said, "Lord, Sister Maureen is not through doing her work here on Earth. You healed her from arthritis so she could carry on with your work and, Lord, I still have my children to raise and I want to share your love with them." I asked God to please get us home safe. I wanted to be home and be with my children.

Unexpectedly, I saw a man in front of me. He was wearing overalls and a shirt. He had on a hat and was barefoot. He was jogging just ahead of my car. He wasn't running fast but was keeping up a slow pace. He waved at me to follow him. I said, "Sister, do you see that man in front of the car?" She said, "No, Sally, I don't see anyone, anywhere." And I said, "Look! Right in front of us! There's a man and he wants us to follow him." Sister then said, "Sally, are you going to hit him?" I said, "No, I'm not going to hit him, Sister, but he's telling me to follow him." I never saw this man's face but only saw his arms wave at me to follow him, and I saw that his feet were bare. I remember that I kept going and going and telling Sister, "I see him, Sister, I'm following him." She kept praying the Rosary. I don't know if she thought I was nuts, or what.

Then, all at once, the fog lifted and the man disappeared into the fog. It seemed as though he ran off to the side of the highway. I could no longer see him, but I began to see other cars at that point. I could see light, the white line, headlights, and tail lights. I said, "Thank you, Jesus. Thank you." I said, "Sister, that was Jesus." She never said a word. Whether she believed me, I may never know.

Psalm 121:1-8 says:

> I raise my eyes toward the mountains.
> From where will my help come?
> My help comes from the LORD,
> the maker of heaven and earth.
> God will not allow your foot to slip,
> your guardian does not sleep.
> Truly, the guardian of Israel
> never slumbers nor sleeps.
> The LORD is your guardian;
> the LORD is your shade
> at your right hand.
> By day the sun cannot harm you,
> nor the moon by night.
> The LORD will guard you from all evil,
> will always guard your life.
> The LORD will guard your coming and going
> both now and forever.

Living the Sorrowful Mysteries

We might not ever fully comprehend the anguish our Lord endured when He went out into the desert for forty days and forty nights, neither might we ever possibly relate to the abandonment and torment He suffered while on His way to death. How might we experience one splinter of pain from the cross He carried or the nails that pierced his flesh? How might we place ourselves at the foot of the cross? Well, you may say, there's no need to place ourselves at the foot of the cross or be concerned with a splinter of suffering. After all, Jesus died once for all mankind, and there is no need to dwell on His suffering. It is finished. He has resurrected, and we are saved through the blood of the Lamb. Indeed, we are saved through the blood of the Lamb. Yet, it is the image of the slain Lamb, Jesus, who keeps us whole and fills us with faith, love, and hope.

The marks of Christ's suffering are enough to make us fall to our knees and cry out like St. Thomas, "My Lord and my God." Jesus is God and, as God, He was able to resurrect and He could have chosen to erase the scars of his sacrifice. Instead, Jesus chose to keep his wounds visible. Why? Our Savior knows our weaknesses, so He chose to leave an everlasting image of suffering—an image that continues to transform lives. His wounds show how much He loves us.

Meditating on Christ's suffering is an immense act of love and a powerful form of prayer, which can uplift us spiritually. There is another form of meditative prayer, which is simple, yet phenomenally mystical, and one that Christians have uttered for more than eight hundred years—The Holy Rosary.

It was 1980, and the season of Lent was upon us again. I decided to spend the forty days praying the Sorrowful Mysteries of the Rosary. I wanted to be close to our Lord and partake in His suffering. I wanted to be at the foot of the cross.

Every night I fell to my knees, closed my eyes, and strummed my fingers across my little wooden beads. I repeatedly whispered the Lord's Prayer and repeated the words the angel Gabriel spoke to Mary, "Hail, Mary, full of grace, the Lord is with thee," as well as the words that Elizabeth spoke to Mary, "Oh, blessed are thou among women and blessed is the fruit of thy womb."

The sorrowful mysteries tell the story of our Lord's passion beginning in the Garden of Gethsemane and ending with His last breath as he prayed, "Father, forgive them, they know not what they do." I continually prayed that Jesus would reveal Himself to me.

One Lenten evening, after I completed my household chores, I retired to my room and knelt at my altar. I picked up my rosary, looked up at the crucifix, and began to pray: "In the name of the Father, and of the Son, and of the Holy Spirit." I closed my eyes and began to meditate on the first Sorrowful Mystery. An interior locution began to unfold like a movie in my mind, and I saw a moon-lit garden of trees and large rocks. There, just beyond the shadows, leaning up against a rock knelt Jesus in intense prayer. His long and dusty robe, ripped at the knee, was visible under the moonlight. I continued to pray in silence, as my spiritual eyes remained wide open watching our Lord in His anguish. Dark drops of sweat, like blood, fell from his brow. I watched at a short distance. He paused. He looked up and then turned His beautiful eyes toward mine. Then, with a most piercing deep gaze, filled with love and mercy, He spoke loud and clear, yet not with His lips. In some mystical way, his eyes spoke—*this is how much I love you.*

As I prayed the second mystery of the Rosary, I was ever present as the soldiers confronted Jesus. An altercation began, and utter chaos ensued with me in the midst. Our precious Lord was dragged and kicked. Loud jeering followed, and the tormentors did not let Him rest or catch His breath. They slapped his face, others spat at him, and the more they tortured Him, the more they cheered and laughed. In the midst of this pandemonium, our Lord's precious eyes gazed into mine. He wept with compassion for His tormentors—"Forgive them. I forgive you." I was there. I was witness to the sounds, the smells, the dust, the blood, the anger, the sorrow, and the love. I felt the heart of the tormentors' rage as if I was one of them.

I continued to pray and meditate on the third and fourth mysteries of the Rosary. The revelation was unlike a vivid dream. The events were real and continued to unfold as I was in the midst of the crowd of people gathered around Jesus, their clothes old and tattered. We laughed and taunted Jesus and one another, "He says He's the King of the Jews. Get a crown on His head. Over there, get the branch with thorns; pull it together." One of them formed a bramble branch into a crown, lifted it, and placed it on our Lord's head. Another turned and snarled at Jesus. The former then noticed the crown was much too small, so he forcibly thrust it down upon our Lord's head causing our Lord to close his precious eyes and shiver in utter anguish. Blood immediately flowed from his pierced head, brow, and temples. I could no longer restrain my sorrow, I cried out, "Lord, oh my Lord." He gazed into my eyes with His loving, tacit response,

"Don't worry. I love you, I forgive you. I suffer for you." I knew at that moment that He suffered not only for me, but also for each one of us as if we were the only one.

I could feel the rosary beads in my hand. My tears flowed, yet I continued to pray. I remained in an ecstatic state, completely partaking in our Lord's suffering. My sins and I weighed heavy on His cross. He struggled in pain yet refused to let go of the cross. As He willfully pushed his body forward, he glanced back at me and said, "I love you. I have forgiven your sins." Words could not describe the love in His eyes. We reached the top of a rocky hill called Golgotha. I looked at my hands and I held a large rugged spike similar to those that attach railroad tracks. Our Lord willfully laid his body down on the cross. I held the metal spike in place so that the soldier could hammer it into our Lord's wrist. I was tormented within and could hear him say, "This must be done." A soldier slammed the large hammer down upon the nail, and it ripped through His flesh. As they raised Him up on the cross, His eyes continued to follow me. Another soldier walked by and suddenly thrashed a lance through our Lord's right side, immediately causing a burst of water and blood to splatter and flow. This horrific image somehow imparted a sense of overwhelming joy.

Within the blood and water, which flowed from Jesus' side, I saw my own baptism and heard a voice, "Welcome to my family." Blessed Mother Mary spoke with gentle tenderness, "Look, here is your brother, follow Him and He will lead you to the kingdom." Her words opened my eyes to a simple fact;

my baptism brought me into His family. Of course, He is my brother. Gratefully, I looked up at our Lord, my brother, and saw that the water flowing from His side was glistening like millions of tiny diamonds. Words cannot express the glory of a suffering that reopened the gates of Heaven. The millions of tiny diamonds, beyond brilliance, infused with the gifts of the Holy Spirit, are the same diamonds our priests call upon when praying to transform common water into holy water. In other words, the water that gushed from the side of Christ two thousand years ago is the same water that transforms, at baptism, the newly elect into holy Christian soldiers. Hence, we are all connected in this spiritual realm. This connection extends further when Jesus gave up His Spirit to the Father and broke bread with His brothers, His disciples, thus instituting the Sacrament of the Eucharist—Jesus.

I continued to pray at the foot of the cross. I saw an image of a priest with a cross mark on his hand, which tells me priests are not only called and anointed, but also they are *in persona Christi,* empowered and commissioned by God to extol their rights as priest, prophet, and king to their flocks.

What I experienced in this locution was real, and our Lord granted me a mental image, a synopsis of how we are connected with our Creator. Because our human language is so very limited, I pray that this image will help you to understand the Sorrowful Mysteries.

"The Holy Sacraments"
Illustrated by Pat Wilke Tadena

Soledad (Sally) H. Juarez & Sally Ann Quinones

11
Decade of the Rosary
and
Mother's Death

It is with God's everlasting grace in action that I am able to write about both my mother's and daughter's passing in the last two chapters of my book.

In December of 2004, after suffering for three years, my mother passed away peacefully. She was a very strong woman. I remember very clearly when we were growing up, she always made sure our family had whatever we needed. She nursed my father back to health after he suffered a few strokes.

In 2002, my sister Mary and I started to notice that mom was becoming very forgetful and disoriented. Mom would often drive to visit Mary but was having problems finding her way home. The same route she took for many decades with no problems was at times unrecognizable to her. It was when my sister Mary discovered that mom had not paid her water bill for months that we suspected the worst. Mary called a family meeting and told us that we better take the car keys away from mom. Mom had been calling Mary from different parts of town needing directions to get back home. We finally had to sell her car, so she would stop asking for the keys. Shortly thereafter, our seventy-nine-year-old mother was diagnosed with Alzheimer's. A different type of Alzheimer's had caused the death of her fifty-year-old brother Vince years before.

I lived a few blocks from my mother's home and would visit her most every day. I would ask her for prayers and share my worries with her about my daughter Shelby who was a drug addict. I remember once when I went to her house, she was busy cleaning her cherished knickknacks that she kept in a beautiful cabinet in her living room. I walked in, and she immediately stopped what she was doing and asked me, "What's wrong, Sally?" She could see on my face that something was causing me terrible grief. I got down on my knees and put my head in her lap. I asked her to forgive me for anything I may have ever done to hurt her. As I cried, she held my face with one hand and ran her fingers through my hair with the other. She said, "You have always been a good girl. Don't cry. You haven't hurt me in any way."

I couldn't understand why my prayers were not answered, and why I had to go through so much pain with Shelby's addictions. I felt helpless. I loved her so much. I just didn't know where to turn for help. I told my mother, "I pray and pray, and nothing helps. Mom, what should I do?" She replied, "Pray some more and ask God to give you strength. Do not give up. God does hear your prayers, and He will answer you in His time." I remembered feeling relief just being there with my head on her lap. She comforted me with her absolute love for me and for Shelby. "Don't give up!" Those words still give me strength today to continue on with my life's prayerful journey.

My mother's Alzheimer's was getting worse. That, combined with diabetes complications, prompted my sister Mary to invite mom to live with her and her husband Julian. Concerned with mom's well-being, they could keep a watchful eye over her in their home. Soon after mom settled into Mary and Julian's, my older sister Louise came from Orange County, CA, to visit. During Louise's stay, they decided to plant flowers in the back yard, since mom thoroughly enjoyed gardening. While sitting in the yard and watching my sisters garden, mom fell from the chair and had a seizure. My sisters took her to St. Joseph's Medical Center. After many tests, the doctor told my sisters that mom's kidneys had gotten worse. The doctor made arrangements with a kidney specialist to see us in his office. The specialist told us that mom needed kidney dialysis immediately. We had many questions and concerns, and he answered them all. Afterward, my sister Mary called another family meeting. We all decided that if dialysis would prolong mom's life, that is what we all wanted for her. When we all met with mom, she made it clear that she did not want dialysis and that she wanted to die on God's time. My sister Mary asked her to please do dialysis for us, since we were not ready to let her go. Mom agreed, not for herself, but for her children.

My sister Mary is the youngest daughter, and she and mom shared a very special bond, so I knew she wanted to please her.

Mom chose Mary to make all medical decisions. Early on, the three of us went to a lawyer and had all the papers drawn up and signed. We respected mom's wishes, just as we had promised. Dialysis treatment started once all legalities were settled. We would take turns sitting with mom during treatments to keep her calm, since she cried from the pain and discomfort. I always thought because of the Alzheimer's that she'd be unaware of the situation and pain, but quite the opposite was true.

Watching mom suffer through dialysis to keep her alive for us became cumbersome. We would read and talk to her about her grandchildren, even though she had forgotten their names. The grandchildren would come often to visit. You could see that she recognized them as family because she greeted them with her warm, gentle smile. She would ask, "What is your mother's name?" She had twenty-nine grandchildren, so it was understandable that she couldn't remember their names. What was so amazing to us was that she never forgot her own children's names.

My brother, Louis, is the youngest sibling and only son. The incredible bond that my mom and brother shared was always amazing. Louis' wife, Helen, is a sister to all of us and has always been there for our entire family. Before we moved mom to Mary's house, Helen and Louis, who lived in the home next door to mom, became her daily caregivers. However, we also had to hire professional caregivers because administering prescribed medicines made it difficult at times to handle mom. Lo and behold, when we thought we had all bases covered, mom would fire the caregivers and insist on taking care of herself. Mom's strength and steadfastness never changed. She did not want strangers around her, and that was that! Her dialysis continued for eight months, then she fell ill and was hospitalized again. It was at that time she begged us to let her go to be with our father who died many years before.

My sister called me at work one day and asked me to come to the hospital, so we could make some new decisions. When I arrived, I noticed mom had a black eye, and she was begging to be taken off dialysis and allowed to go be with my dad. The doctor soon arrived, and again mom told him, "I don't want dialysis. Please, let me die. I want to go be with my husband, Louie. I'm tired and don't want to have anymore of anything." I felt her pleas to die deep inside me. The doctor asked who was in charge of mom's medical decisions. The time had come for Mary to put mom's legal desires into action. Mary waited for all of us to arrive before deciding to transfer her to a hospice.

The hospice facility was newly constructed and very nice. A short time after mom was settled in, the day came when we all were to gather around her during her last hours. When I arrived, she explained about her black eye, saying, "I fell, Mia, I fell." She was so very peaceful and happy. She understood that it wouldn't be long before her kidneys would fail her body. She was happy to know she would soon be with God and her husband. We all knew that the end was near, but there was an incredible peace about the entire situation. Family members were arriving to hug her for the last time. The room filled to capacity. It was a joyous time. Mom was very alert and talking. She had no problem recalling names, even grandchildren's nicknames. It was a beautiful send-off to heaven for everyone present.

The hospice nurses treated mom with so much kindness. Mom would smile at them when they did any little thing to make her comfortable. My niece Alice, called Lecha, is a registered nurse and she stayed by mom's side monitoring her blood pressure and heart rate. Finally, Lecha informed us that the end was near. She asked that only the immediate family stay, but that the others step outside to the waiting room where the hospice had provided cookies and juice.

Once everyone was settled in, Mary asked me to lead us in reciting the Rosary. It was a complete blessing to be asked to pray the Rosary at mom's bedside. My sister Carmen, who is a devout Jehovah's Witness, excused herself until we finished praying. Once we began reciting the Rosary, my mother fell into a coma. She was peaceful, as if sleeping comfortably and pain free. I prayed the Glorious Mysteries and, with each decade, I would speak about parts of our lives—how she cared for us, how she accepted us for who we were, how she suffered much to make us a home when we were young. We all asked her to forgive us of any hurt we may have caused. Mom suffered in silence, never complaining. We told her that we would always remember that she never forgot our names. She knew us inside and out. It reminds me of this scripture from Isaiah 49:15, which reads:

"Can a mother forget her infant,
be without tenderness for the child of her womb?
Even should she forget,
I will never forget you."

It was during the last decade of the Rosary when we noticed that mom was taking her last breaths, so we called our
sister Carmen back into the room. Once we all were around
her saying our good-byes, she drew in her last breath, and her
spirit passed on. My sister Mary, who had made all the decisions, leaned over and gave her a big hug. She said, "We all
love you, we are going to miss you, but you go now and be
with Daddy." There was holiness in the room. My sister Carmen who suffers from arthritis in her hands said, "Look at my
hands. I can move my fingers!" She kept looking at her hands
and said again, "They don't hurt. I can move them!"

I know Carmen received a touch of grace in that room. I
believe that the room was filled with angels escorting mom to
the room that God had prepared for her. Mom went to heaven
on December 31, 2004.

John 14:2-3 reads:

In my Father's house there are many dwelling places. If
there were not, would I have told you that I am going
to prepare a place for you? And if I go and prepare a
place for you, I will come back again and take you to
myself so that where I am you also may be.

Shelby Ann Quinones (Shelbo)
Born June 21, 1968
Entered into Rest February 19, 2006

12

Losing a Child
~Shelby's Story~

This chapter is about my daughter Shelby, introduced to you in chapter ten. As you know, she was healed of epilepsy when she was nine years old.

On May 17, 2005, Shelby was released from her fifth or sixth drug rehab center. Three years prior to that time, I had taken care of her two teenage daughters, Ashlee and Kristina. Their grandmother Lucita also helped by picking them up from school every day and bringing them home. I got out of work at five o'clock, so that was a great help.

Shelby was mother to four children. Her boys are Christopher and Anthony. Since I could not care for all four children while she was in rehab, others who loved them dearly cared for the boys. Ashlee, being the eldest, would always make arrangements to have them all come and spend weekends with us. We went to visit Shelby as often as the rehab facility would allow. Once Shelby was out of the rehab center, the girls were thrilled to be reunited with their mom. Shelby seemed to be well on her way to a full recovery—one day at a time. She was so happy to be full-time mom to her daughters and sons. She found a job. In fact, she had two jobs to make ends meet. Shelby needed help to get started in her own rental again, so I was able to buy her some used furniture and other necessary items. She also made arrangements to go back to college. Shelby desired to become a Certified Public Accountant.

A few days before July 4, 2005, I received a call from my daughter Cynthia who went with her husband Danny to Arizona to visit her sister Esther and family. Cynthia asked me, "Why don't you come to Arizona? We found a perfect home for you." I had vacation time, so off to Arizona I went. My son-in-law Ron, Esther's husband, was anxious to show me the property, which was located very close to their home. When we arrived at the home, the owner was watching us through the door. He said, "If you're coming to see the house, it's sold." He continued to say, "The investors signed a contract with me."

The owner remembered Ronnie from the day before, and he allowed us to walk through the home after all, so I would have an opportunity to see it. Ronnie works in real estate and is very familiar with how some investors are known to deal with property owners. Once I had seen the house with my daughters and their husbands, I agreed with them—it was perfect for me! It was big enough to have my children and grandchildren come to visit with enough room to spare. The owner mentioned how sorry he felt, because had I been there just the day before, perhaps I could have put an offer on it. As we turned to leave, Ron said, "I'm going to give you my card just in case the investors change their minds." As I sat in the car, I quietly prayed, "Lord, if it is your will that I have this beautiful home, please make it happen. It's in your hands." My mother had left each of us a little money, and I wanted to use it to buy a home.

The next day, Sunday, I planned to leave on a six o'clock flight. As we were having dinner, Ronnie came into the dining room and said, "The homeowner just called and wants you to make an offer. The investor's contract is null and void." I immediately went to his house and made a formal offer, even leaving him a good-faith check. He told me that he would run a credit check and call me on Monday. I prayed and trusted the Lord with my life for all these years, and it was time to put my faith in action once more.

The time came to make the big move to my new home in Arizona. I was excited and ready to be on my own. I remember everyone came to see me the day before I left. They all looked so happy. I also went to see Shelby at her work one more time before I actually left for Arizona. She was crying and begging me not to move away from her. It made me feel sad, but I said, "Shelby, I have done everything I could to help you. You have your boyfriend Rex and his family. You will be fine." She was always the type of young woman that needed love and reassurance. She had to learn to become the person God created her to be. I'll never forget that sad look on her face. My daughter was always on the honor roll. She was very smart and a beautiful woman. Shelby had a kind heart and wanted to be good but, in the past, the drugs controlled her. Sometimes I think back and wish that if I had only known what the future held, maybe I could have helped her for another year.

In September of 2005, God had another plan for me. Only a few months after arriving in Arizona, I started experiencing chest pains. In December, I became very ill. The discomfort had progressed to the point where I couldn't walk without gasping for air. My son-in-law's mother, Olga Rodriguez, told me about Mission of Mercy Bus that traveled to different locations to provide health care for people without insurance. Thankfully, Dr. Smith, who was in charge of the Mission of Mercy, was a retired cardiologist. My ongoing symptoms prompted him to suggest I receive more extensive care to avoid a possible heart attack. However, later that month, I went back to Stockton to visit with my children. More important, I needed to check-in with Shelby.

Shelby looked tired from working two jobs, but she genuinely seemed happy. She and the family had plans to go to her boyfriend's family retreat in the mountains. I asked her what she wanted for Christmas, and she mentioned she needed pants. Her boyfriend Rex, however, asked her to wear a dress for the holidays. I decided to buy her a dress, which made Rex very happy.

During my visit in Stockton, I didn't tell anyone about the heart trouble I was experiencing. Christmas turned out to be a joyous time for my entire family.

Once I returned home from California, I had to go back to the Mercy Mission Bus to get more medicine for my heart. I really did not understand why I was feeling so poorly until February. Dr. Smith ordered an EKG, and the results were not good. In fact, Dr. Smith was extremely concerned for my life. I lied to him and told him that my eldest daughter, Cynthia, was coming to stay with me. The truth was that she was only coming for a visit. She came for a week, so I could pray over her feet. They had been causing her extreme discomfort, so much, that she was on disability.

On February 19, we were invited to Joe and Olga Rodriguez' home for dinner in Fountain Hills. Olga suggested that Cynthia and I get anointed. I called St. Bridget Church where I was an active member of the congregation at that time. I didn't think the priest would do it the same day, but he agreed to anoint us both after five o'clock Mass. I remember feeling God's presence surround us in a special way. After the anointing, we all went to Ronnie and Esther's house for dessert. As we were sitting around the table visiting, I noticed Cynthia and Esther going up and down the stairs. One after the other was speaking on the phone. I remember thinking something must be wrong.

Both my daughters came directly over to me and said, "Mom we have some very bad news to tell you. Shelby has committed suicide." I couldn't move. I just sat there. Then I started hitting the chair next to me. I was in complete shock. I thought, *What happened? I just saw her and she looked so good. God what happened? Why Lord? Why wasn't I there with her?* You ask yourself so many questions. So much guilt rushed through my mind. My baby girl was gone. I wasn't there to help her. I could not stop crying.

Shelby had left a note in the front yard not to open the garage. To this day, I do not know the details, but I believe her pain was manifesting in my heart. God knew that my heart was going to be broken. Shelby died at 5:22 that afternoon, which was the same time I was attending Mass with my daughter Cynthia. Again, I believe God's everlasting grace was in action.

The anointing that I received that day is what got me through the pain of losing Shelby. I was able to speak at my daughter's funeral with my son Rudy standing at my side. After a week in California and dealing with the funeral arrangements, I returned back home to Arizona. The night I arrived home, I was praying when I saw Shelby in a vision. She was wearing a pink grown and her hands were in a praying position. God's white light surrounded her. I said her name aloud, then she was gone. I am very thankful to God that I saw her in a very clear vision. She looked like she did when she was about fifteen years old. I believe the Lord allowed me to see her in a very peaceful state where the demons could not entice her any longer. I believe that she suffered a relapse and just could not face the reality that her kids would be taken from her, and that the guilt of letting herself and others down was too much for her to bear. Drugs are so damaging.

That was a sad time in my life, but life does go on. Children are to bury their parents, not parents to bury their children. Shelby is greatly missed by all of us. Sometimes we get together and talk about the good times when she was young and innocent.

I found it very hard to write about my daughter and tell the truth about her passing. For years, when people asked how my daughter died, I would tell them she died from an aneurysm. I couldn't speak the word suicide. I could not utter that horrible word through my lips. I carried so much guilt that it wasn't until I went to the Christ Renews His Parish retreat in April of 2009, that I was finally freed of the guilt through God's amazing healing. I confessed my guilt to Father Peter Dai Bui. I hope he realizes the freedom I received that night during reconciliation. Since that retreat, I was asked to speak at future retreats to help others. I share my story about the Eucharist and, at the last retreat, I shared about my daughter's suicide. I now believe that if this story can help someone, then I will share it.

I thank God that he gave me the opportunity to be honest. Before I wrote this book, only a few people knew Shelby's story, and now everyone will know. Life does go on for me, but there is an empty space in my heart. My faith keeps me going, and I truly believe that I will see Shelby in Heaven one day.

Psalms 139:1-12 reads:

> LORD, you have probed me, you know me:
> you know when I sit and stand;
> you understand my thoughts from afar.
> …Where can I hide from your spirit?
> From your presence, where can I flee?
> If I ascend to the heavens, you are there;
> if I lie down in Sheol, you are there too.
> If I fly with the wings of dawn
> and alight beyond the sea,
> Even there your hand will guide me,
> your right hand hold me fast.
> If I say, "Surely darkness shall hide me,
> and night shall be my light"—
> Darkness is not dark for you,
> and night shines as the day.
> Darkness and light are but one.

My Prayer List

My Prayer List

_____

_____

_____

_____

_____

_____

_____

_____

_____

_____

_____

_____

_____

_____

_____

_____

_____

_____

_____

_____

_____

_____

_____

_____